Be Revolutionary

Some Thoughts from Pope Francis

Other Books by Glenn Alan Cheney

Law of the Jungle:
Environmental Anarchy and the Tenharim People of Amazonia

Quilombo dos Palmares:
Brazil's Lost Nation of Fugitive Slaves

Ex Cathedra: Stories by Machado de Assis

How a Nation Grieves: Press Accounts of the Death of Lincoln,
the Hunt for Booth, and America in Mourning

Thanksgiving:
The Pilgrims' First Year in America

Journey on the Estrada Real:
Encounters in the Mountains of Brazil

Journey to Chernobyl:
Encounters in a Radioactive Zone

Promised Land:
A Nun's Struggle against Landlessness, Lawlessness, Slavery, Poverty,
Corruption, and Environmental Devastation in Amazonia

Love and Death in the Kingdom of Swaziland

Frankenstein on the Cusp of Something

Passion in an Improper Place

Acts of Ineffable Love: Collected Stories

Poems Askance

Neighborhood News

Life in Caves

Be Revolutionary

Some Thoughts from Pope Francis

Glenn Alan Cheney
Editor

New London Librarium
Hanover, Conn.

Be Revolutionary:
Some Thoughts from Pope Francis
Second Edition

Editor: Glenn Alan Cheney
with a Foreword by
Sr. Barbara Staley, MSC

New London Librarium
P.O. Box 284
18 Parkwood
Hanover, CT 06350
NLLibrarium.com

Copyright © 2015 Libreria Editrice Vaticana
Copyright © 2015 Glenn Alan Cheney

Back cover photo courtesy of Korea.net / Korean Culture and Information Service

All rights reserved.

ISBN

paperback: 978-0-9905899-4-5
             0990589943
eBook: 978-0-9905899-5-2

10 9 8 7 6 5 4 3 2 1

Printed in the United States of America

for
Maria do Carmo Chaves de Sousa Lessa

Some Thoughts from Pope Francis

Contents

Foreword	*vii*
On the Worship of Money	3
On Grassroots Organizations	4
On Solidarity	5
On Social Activists	6
On Altruism and Hypocrisy	7
On Land	8
On Housing	9
On Real Estate	10
On Slums	11
On Work	12
On Exploitation	13
On the Value of Workers	14
On the Discarding of People	15
On Unemployment	16
On the War Industry	18
On the Plunder of Nature	19
On Integrating the Local and the Global	20
On Grassroots Movements	21
On the Cost of Consumerism	22
On the Loss of Happiness	23
On the Spreading of Goodness	24
On the Economy of Exclusion	25
On People as Leftovers	26
On Trickle-down Economics	27
On the Financial Crisis	28
On the Wealth Gap	29
On Ethics	30
On Inequality	31
On Religious Freedom	32
On Superficial Culture	33

i

On the Rejection of the Transcendent	*34*
On The Cultural Crisis within Families	*35*
On Urban Crime	*36*
On Christian Service	*37*
On Liberation Communication	*38*
On the Quest for Spirituality	*39*
On Talk	*40*
On the Liberation and Promotion of the Poor	*41*
On the Social Function of Property	*42*
On the Rights of All Peoples	*43*
On Labor Disparity	*44*
On the Elderly	*45*
On Religious Freedom	*46*
On Attitudes for Religious Freedom	*47*
On Remedying the Causes of Poverty	*48*
On Irksome Discourse	*49*
On Market Forces	*50*
On Politicians	*51*
On Global Economics	*52*
On Papal Interest	*53*
On the Defense of Species	*54*
On the Nature of Peace	*55*
On Time and Space	*56*
On Ideas and Realities	*57*
On Globalization and Localization	*58*
On Relations with Islam	*59*
On Embracing Muslims	*60*
On Mary	*61*
On Fear of Freedom	*62*
On Migrants and Refugees	*63*
On Slaves	*64*
On the Causes of Slavery	*66*
On the Seeking of Truth	*68*

Some Thoughts from Pope Francis

On Religious Freedom	69
On Financial Markets	70
On Legacy	71
On the Courage to Make Peace	72
On Expectations of the G20	73
On ISIS	74
On Global Warming	75
On Dialogue with Other Religions	76
On Grandparents	77
On the Olympics	78
On Hidden Slavery	79
On Islamophobia	80
On Christianophobia	81
On His Prayer in a Mosque	82
On the Ongoing Third World War	83
On Atomic Weapons	84
On Middle East Peace	85
On Hunger	86
On Solidarity and Hunger	87
On the Concept of Person	88
On Dignity and Economic Interests	89
On Individual Rights and Duties	90
On Loneliness	91
On Transcendence of Heaven and Earth	92
On Stewardship of Nature	93
On Christians as a Soul	94
On Experimentation with Life	95
On Economy and Finance	96
On Religious Diversity	97
On Rugby	98
On Torture	99
On Stopping Aggressors	100
On Diplomacy	101

On the Work of Justice	*102*
On Cultivation	*103*
On Playing with Children	*104*
On Unemployment	*105*
On Pilgrims	*106*
On Learning	*107*
On Education	*108*
On Hope	*109*
On Homosexuality	*110*
On Soccer	*111*
On Healthcare	*112*
On Right to Life	*113*
On Economy and Morality	*114*
On Abuse of Children by Priests	*115*
On Educational Experimentation	*116*
On New Culture	*117*
On Human Trafficking	*118*
On Mayors	*119*
On His Own Happiness	*120*
On Work	*121*
On Unemployment	*122*
On Marriage Forever	*123*
On Jorge Mario Bergoglio	*124*
Laudato Si: Encyclical on Care of Our Common Home (excerpts)	*127*
Sources	*193*
About Pope Francis	*199*
About Sister Barbara Staley	*200*
About Glenn Alan Cheney	*201*

Some Thoughts from Pope Francis

Be Revolutionary

Some Thoughts from Pope Francis

Foreword

Glenn Cheney's compilation of Pope Francis's words needs no explanation. What the Pope says, speaks for itself. Or does it? It is easy to make an intellectual assent to words on paper. Applying those words into our everyday lives is much more challenging. If there is no application of the written word into a lived experience, then the words become meaningless.

Pope Francis speaks of the everyday life that resonates in all of us. His actions bespeak those of a prophet. The Catholic hierarchical Church has long focused on the "law" and asserted its teaching authority. This was a proper role. But Pope Francis is bringing a new dimension to his Hierarchical role, that of merging a prophetic voice into his teachings. In both the Hebrew Scriptures and the New Testament, the role of the prophet has been to speak an important message from God to a people. A prophet speaks on behalf of God about real problems, real social phenomena. The prophet relays God's love for people — all people, not just some. God is impartial in His extravagant love, and He wants us, too, to be extravagant in expressing love to all people.

The Pope demonstrates a profound human integration. When asked who he is, Francis states simply, "I am a sinner." He knows (and upholds) the Church's teachings. He also knows human frailty and the richness of God's mercy. So when Pope Francis is asked about suffering by a twelve-year-old child in the Philippines, he doesn't give a theological treatise. Rather, he hugs her and says he doesn't understand either.

He knows that actions speak about love more strongly than words. When asked about homosexuality, the Pope replies, "If someone is gay and searches for the Lord and has goodwill, who am I to judge?" He eschews privilege with simple gestures such as wearing old shoes, and standing in line at a hotel to pay his bill.

The gift God is giving us through this leader of the Catholic Church is a man who names social evils yet believes that transformative love can replace those evils with social good and with God's love. Francis focuses the Gospel into concrete actions. He tells us what love and Love look like, and he challenges us to respond, too. And in the end that's what love and Love are all about.

As a Missionary Sister of the Sacred Heart of Jesus, I spent my life offering professional skill to help the real, concrete needs of people marginalized from society because of poverty, disability, legal status, homelessness, sexual orientation, AIDS, violence, ignorance, addictions, age, and other challenges. As I dedicate my life to this effort, the Holy Father reaches out to me with his words and gestures. They reach out to me and assure me that my work has been a proper practice and preaching of the Gospel. But his words also call me to give more.

For ten years I worked in Swaziland taking care of people with AIDS and helping their children, families and communities. There were moments during those years that Sr. Diane Dalle Molle, MSC, and I would stop and wonder if we should be doing more direct evangelization in our ministry. We asked ourselves, are we doing enough? Do people know why we are here? Do people know it is because of Jesus that we

Some Thoughts from Pope Francis

are here? I was consoled one day when a young orphaned boy said to me, "You must never leave Sister." I asked why. After a long pause, he shrugged his shoulders and said, "Because God sent you here."

I pray with Pope Francis's words. I hope that they don't remain words on paper but become inspiration to action. I am sure each reader of this small book will find personal inspiration and a call to action. Along with the Pope I am sure of God's extravagant love for each reader and His grace to transform your life bit by bit into one that heeds this papal prophet's call and helps to bring mercy and justice more fully into the world today.

SR. BARBARA STALEY, MSC
Superior General
Missionary Sisters of the Sacred Heart of Jesus
mothercabrini.org
msccabrini.org
Cabriniministries.org

Be Revolutionary

Some Thoughts from Pope Francis

Some Thoughts from Pope Francis

On the Worship of Money

We talk about land, work, housing ... we talk about working for peace and taking care of nature. Why are we accustomed to seeing decent work destroyed, countless families evicted, rural farmworkers driven off the land, war waged and nature abused? Because in this system man, the human person, has been removed from the centre and replaced by something else. Because idolatrous worship is devoted to money. Because indifference has been globalized: "Why should I care what happens to others as long as I can defend what's mine?" Because the world has forgotten God, who is Father; and by setting God aside, it has made itself an orphan.Some of you said that this system cannot endure. We must change it. We must put human dignity back at the centre and on that pillar build the alternative social structures we need. This must be done with courage but also with intelligence, with tenacity but without fanaticism, with passion yet without violence. And all of us together, addressing the conflicts without getting trapped in them, always seeking to resolve the tensions in order to reach a higher plane of unity, of peace and of justice. We Christians have something very lovely, a guide to action, a program we could call revolutionary. I earnestly recommend that you read it: the Beatitudes in Saint Matthew chapter 5, and in Saint Luke chapter 6; and the Last Judgment passage.

On Grassroots Organizations

You [representatives of grassroots organizations] are not satisfied with empty promises, with alibis or excuses. Nor do you wait with arms crossed for non-governmental organizations to help, for welfare schemes or paternalistic solutions that never arrive. Or if they do, then it is with a tendency to anaesthetize or to domesticate ... and this is rather perilous. One senses that the poor are no longer waiting. You want to be protagonists. You get organized, study, work, issue demands and, above all, practice that very special solidarity that exists among those who suffer, among the poor, and that our civilization seems to have forgotten or would strongly prefer to forget.

On Solidarity

Solidarity is a word that is not always well received. In certain circumstances it has become a dirty word, something one dares not say. However, it is a word that means much more than an occasional gesture of generosity. It means thinking and acting in terms of community. It means that the lives of all take priority over the appropriation of goods by a few. It also means fighting against the structural causes of poverty and inequality; of the lack of work, land and housing; and of the denial of social and labour rights. It means confronting the destructive effects of the empire of money: forced dislocation, painful emigration, human trafficking, drugs, war, violence and all those realities that many of you suffer and that we are all called upon to transform. Solidarity, understood in its deepest sense, is a way of making history, and this is what the popular movements are doing.

Be Revolutionary

On Social Activists

You do not work with abstract ideas; you work with realities such as those I just mentioned and many others that you have told me about. You have your feet in the mud, you are up to your elbows in flesh-and-blood reality. Your carry the smell of your neighborhood, your people, your struggle! We want your voices to be heard – voices that are rarely heard. No doubt this is because your voices cause embarrassment, no doubt it is because your cries are bothersome, no doubt because people are afraid of the change that you seek. However, without your presence, without truly going to the fringes, the good proposals and projects we often hear about at international conferences remain stuck in the realm of ideas and wishful thinking.

Some Thoughts from Pope Francis

On Altruism and Hypocrisy

The scandal of poverty cannot be addressed by promoting strategies of containment that only tranquilize the poor and render them tame and inoffensive. How sad it is when we find, behind allegedly altruistic works, the other being reduced to passivity or being negated; or worse still, we find hidden personal agendas or commercial interests. "Hypocrites" is what Jesus would say to those responsible. How marvelous it is, by contrast, when we see peoples moving forward, especially their young and their poorest members. Then one feels a promising breeze that revives hope for a better world. May this breeze become a cyclone of hope. This is my wish.

On Land

Land. At the beginning of creation, God created man and woman, stewards of his work, mandating them to till and to keep it. I want to congratulate farm workers — *campesinos* — for caring for the land, for cultivating it and for doing so in community. The elimination of so many brothers and sisters campesinos worries me, and it is not because of wars or natural disasters that they are uprooted. Land and water grabbing, deforestation, unsuitable pesticides are some of the evils which uproot people from their native land. This wretched separation is not only physical but existential and spiritual as well because there is a relationship with the land, such that rural communities and their special way of life are being put at flagrant risk of decline and even of extinction.

The other dimension of this already global process is hunger. When financial speculation manipulates the price of food, treating it as just another commodity, millions of people suffer and die from hunger. At the same time, tons of food are thrown away. This constitutes a genuine scandal. Hunger is criminal, food is an inalienable right.

Some Thoughts from Pope Francis

On Housing

I said it and I repeat it: a home for every family. We must never forget that, because there was no room in the inn, Jesus was born in a stable; and that his family, persecuted by Herod, had to leave their home and flee into Egypt. Today there are so many homeless families, either because they have never had one or because, for different reasons, they have lost it. Family and housing go hand in hand. Furthermore, for a house to be a home, it requires a community dimension, and this is the neighbourhood ... and it is precisely in the neighbourhood where the great family of humanity begins to be built, starting from the most immediate instance, from living together with one's neighbours. We live nowadays in immense cities that show off proudly, even arrogantly, how modern they are. But while they offer wellbeing and innumerable pleasures for a happy minority, housing is denied to thousands of our neighbours, our brothers and sisters including children, who are called elegant names such as "street people" or "without fixed abode" or "urban camper." Isn't it curious how euphemisms abound in the world of injustices! A person, a segregated person, a person set apart, a person who suffers misery or hunger: such a one is "urban camper." It is an elegant expression, isn't it? You should be on the lookout – I might be wrong in some cases; but in general, what lurks behind each euphemism is a crime.

Be Revolutionary

On Real Estate

We live in cities that throw up skyscrapers and shopping centres and strike big real estate deals ... but they abandon a part of themselves to marginal settlements on the periphery. How painful it is to hear that poor settlements are marginalized, or, worse still, earmarked for demolition! How cruel are the images of violent evictions, bulldozers knocking down the tiny dwellings, images just like from a war. And this is what we see today.

Some Thoughts from Pope Francis

On Slums

You know that in the crowded slums where many of you live, values endure that have been forgotten in the rich centres. These settlements are blessed with a rich popular culture where public areas are not just transit corridors but an extension of the home, a place where bonds can be forged with neighbours. How lovely are cities that overcome unhealthy mistrust and integrate those who are different, even making such integration a new factor of development. How lovely are cities that, in their architectural design, are full of spaces that unite, connect and foster recognition of the other. So the line to follow is neither eradication nor marginalization but urban integration. Moreover, not only must the word "integration" replace all talk of eradication; it must also supplant those projects that aim to varnish poor neighborhoods, prettify the outskirts and daub make-up on social ailments instead of curing them by promoting genuine and respectful integration. It is a sort of cosmetic architecture, isn't it? And it is the trend. So let us keep on working so that all families have housing and so that all neighborhoods have adequate infrastructure (sewage, light, gas, asphalted roads); and I go on: schools, hospitals or first aid clinics, sports clubs and all those things that create bonds and unite; and as I have already said, access to health care and to education and to secure tenancy.

On Work

There is no worse material poverty – I really must stress this – there is no worse material poverty than the poverty which does not allow people to earn their bread, which deprives them of the dignity of work. But youth unemployment, informality or underground work, and the lack of labour rights are not inevitable. These are the result of an underlying social choice in favour of an economic system that puts profit above man. If economic profit takes precedence over the individual and over humanity, we find a throw-away culture at work that considers humanity in itself, human beings, as a consumer good, which can be used and then thrown away.

Some Thoughts from Pope Francis

On Exploitation

Today, a new dimension is being added to the phenomena of exploitation and oppression, a very harsh and graphic manifestation of social injustice: those who cannot be integrated, the excluded, are discarded, the "leftovers." This is the throw-away culture, and I would like to add something on this that I just remember now, I do not have it written down. This happens when the deity of money is at the centre of an economic system rather than man, the human person. Yes, at the centre of every social or economic system must be the person, image of God, created to "have dominion over" the universe. The inversion of values happens when the person is displaced and money becomes the deity.

On the Value of Workers

I remember a teaching from around the year 1200 that illustrates this point. A Jewish Rabbi was explaining the story of the Tower of Babel to his faithful. He recounted the extraordinary effort required to build it: the bricks had to be made, and to make the bricks one had to mix mud and fetch straw, knead the mud with the straw, then cut it into squares, then dry them, then fire them, and after the bricks were fired and then cooled, hoist them up to keep on building the tower. If a brick fell – a brick was very costly, given all the work – if a brick fell, it was almost a national tragedy. Whoever dropped it was punished or suspended or whatever. But if a worker fell, nothing happened. That is the situation when the person is at the service of the deity money – so said a Jewish Rabbi in the year 1200 explaining such terrible incidents.

Some Thoughts from Pope Francis

On the Discarding of People

Today children are disposed of because the birth-rate in many of the world's countries has fallen, or because there is no food, or because they are killed before being born – children are thrown away. The elderly are discarded, well, because they are useless, they are not productive. Neither children nor the elderly produce, and so, with more or less sophisticated systems, they are slowly being abandoned. And in the current period of economic crisis, now that it is necessary to regain a certain equilibrium, we are witnessing a third very painful disposal – the disposal of young people. Millions of young people — I do not want to give a precise figure because I do not know the exact number, and what I read seems somewhat inflated — anyhow, millions of young people are discarded from work, are unemployed.

Be Revolutionary

On Unemployment

In European countries where statistics are very clear, and specifically here in Italy, slightly more than 40% of young people are unemployed. Do you know what 40% of young people means? A whole generation is being cancelled, in order to restore the balance sheet. In another European country, it is over 50% and up to 60% in its southern region. These are clear counts of discarded debris. So in addition to discarding children and the elderly who do not produce, a generation of young people is to be sacrificed, people thrown away, in order to prop up and rebalance a system with the deity money at its centre and not the human person.Despite this throw-away culture, this culture of leftovers, so many of you who are excluded workers, the discards of this system, have been inventing your own work with materials that seemed to be devoid of further productive value...

But with the craftsmanship God gave you, with your inventiveness, your solidarity, your community work, your popular economy, you have managed to succeed, you are succeeding... And let me tell you, besides work, this is poetry. I thank you.

From now on every worker, within the formal system of salaried employment or outside it, should have the right to decent remuneration, to social security and to a pension. Among you here are waste-collectors, recyclers, peddlers, seamstresses or tailors, artisans, fishermen, farmworkers, builders, miners, workers in previously abandoned enterprises, members of all kinds of cooperatives and workers in grassroots jobs who are excluded from labour rights, who are denied the possibility of unionizing, whose income is neither adequate nor stable.On Peace and EcologyIt is logical. There cannot be land, there cannot be housing, there cannot be work if we do not have peace and if we destroy the planet. These are such important topics that the peoples of the world and their popular organizations cannot fail to debate them. This cannot just remain in the hands of political leaders. All peoples of the earth, all men and women of good will – all of us must raise our voices in defence of these two precious gifts: peace and nature or "Sister Mother Earth" as Saint Francis of Assisi called her.

On the War Industry

Recently I said and now I repeat, we are going through World War Three but in installments. There are economic systems that must make war in order to survive. Accordingly, arms are manufactured and sold and, with that, the balance sheets of economies that sacrifice man at the feet of the idol of money are clearly rendered healthy. And no thought is given to hungry children in refugee camps; no thought is given to the forcibly displaced; no thought is given to destroyed homes; no thought is given, finally, to so many destroyed lives. How much suffering, how much destruction, how much grief. Today, dear brothers and sisters, in all parts of the earth, in all nations, in every heart and in grassroots movements, the cry wells up for peace: War no more!

Some Thoughts from Pope Francis

On the Plunder of Nature

An economic system centered on the deity money also needs to plunder nature to sustain consumption at the frenetic level it needs. Climate change, the loss of biodiversity, deforestation are already showing their devastating effects in terrible cataclysms which we see and from which you the humble suffer most – you who live near the coast in precarious dwellings, or so economically vulnerable that you lose everything due to a natural disaster. Brothers and sisters, creation is not a possession that we can dispose of as we wish; much less is it the property of some, of only a few. Creation is a gift, it is a present, it is a marvelous gift given to us by God so that we might care for it and use it, always gratefully and always respectfully, for the benefit of everyone.

Be Revolutionary

On Integrating the Local and the Global

I know that you [members of grassroots organizations] are persons of different religions, trades, ideas, cultures, countries, continents. Here and now you are practicing the culture of encounter, so different from the xenophobia, discrimination and intolerance which we witness so often. Among the excluded, one finds an encounter of cultures where the aggregate does not wipe out the particularities. That is why I like the image of the polyhedron, a geometric figure with many different facets. The polyhedron reflects the confluence of all the partialities that in it keep their originality. Nothing is dissolved, nothing is destroyed, nothing is dominated, everything is integrated. Nowadays you too are looking for that synthesis between the local and the global. I know that you work daily in what is close at hand and concrete, in your area, your neighbourhood, your work place. I also invite you to keep seeking that broader perspective so that our dreams might fly high and embrace the whole.

Some Thoughts from Pope Francis

On Grassroots Movements

Grassroots movements express the urgent need to revitalize our democracies, so often hijacked by innumerable factors. It is impossible to imagine a future for society without the active participation of great majorities as protagonists, and such proactive participation overflows the logical procedures of formal democracy. Moving towards a world of lasting peace and justice calls us to go beyond paternalistic forms of assistance; it calls us to create new forms of participation that include popular movements and invigorate local, national and international governing structures with that torrent of moral energy that springs from including the excluded in the building of a common destiny. And all this with a constructive spirit, without resentment, with love.I accompany you wholeheartedly on this journey. From our hearts let us say together: No family without housing, no farmworker without land, no worker without rights, no one without the dignity that work provides.

On the Cost of Consumerism

The great danger in today's world, pervaded as it is by consumerism, is the desolation and anguish born of a complacent yet covetous heart, the feverish pursuit of frivolous pleasures, and a blunted conscience. Whenever our interior life becomes caught up in its own interests and concerns, there is no longer room for others, no place for the poor. God's voice is no longer heard, the quiet joy of his love is no longer felt, and the desire to do good fades.

Some Thoughts from Pope Francis

On the Loss of Happiness

There are Christians whose lives seem like Lent without Easter. I realize of course that joy is not expressed the same way at all times in life, especially at moments of great difficulty. Joy adapts and changes, but it always endures, even as a flicker of light born of our personal certainty that, when everything is said and done, we are infinitely loved....

Sometimes we are tempted to find excuses and complain, acting as if we could only be happy if a thousand conditions were met. To some extent this is because our "technological society has succeeded in multiplying occasions of pleasure, yet has found it very difficult to engender joy." I can say that the most beautiful and natural expressions of joy which I have seen in my life were in poor people who had little to hold on to. I also think of the real joy shown by others who, even amid pressing professional obligations, were able to preserve, in detachment and simplicity, a heart full of faith.

Be Revolutionary

On the Spreading of Goodness

Goodness always tends to spread. Every authentic experience of truth and goodness seeks by its very nature to grow within us, and any person who has experienced a profound liberation becomes more sensitive to the needs of others. As it expands, goodness takes root and develops. If we wish to lead a dignified and fulfilling life, we have to reach out to others and seek their good.

Some Thoughts from Pope Francis

On the Economy of Exclusion

Just as the commandment "Thou shalt not kill" sets a clear limit in order to safeguard the value of human life, today we also have to say "thou shalt not" to an economy of exclusion and inequality. Such an economy kills. How can it be that it is not a news item when an elderly homeless person dies of exposure, but it is news when the stock market loses two points? This is a case of exclusion. Can we continue to stand by when food is thrown away while people are starving? This is a case of inequality. Today everything comes under the laws of competition and the survival of the fittest, where the powerful feed upon the powerless. As a consequence, masses of people find themselves excluded and marginalized: without work, without possibilities, without any means of escape.

On People as Leftovers

Human beings are themselves considered consumer goods to be used and then discarded. We have created a "throw away" culture which is now spreading. It is no longer simply about exploitation and oppression, but something new. Exclusion ultimately has to do with what it means to be a part of the society in which we live; those excluded are no longer society's underside or its fringes or its disenfranchised – they are no longer even a part of it. The excluded are not the "exploited" but the outcast, the "leftovers."

Some Thoughts from Pope Francis

On Trickle-down Economics

Some people continue to defend trickle-down theories which assume that economic growth, encouraged by a free market, will inevitably succeed in bringing about greater justice and inclusiveness in the world. This opinion, which has never been confirmed by the facts, expresses a crude and naïve trust in the goodness of those wielding economic power and in the sacralized workings of the prevailing economic system. Meanwhile, the excluded are still waiting. To sustain a lifestyle which excludes others, or to sustain enthusiasm for that selfish ideal, a globalization of indifference has developed. Almost without being aware of it, we end up being incapable of feeling compassion at the outcry of the poor, weeping for other people's pain, and feeling a need to help them, as though all this were someone else's responsibility and not our own. The culture of prosperity deadens us; we are thrilled if the market offers us something new to purchase. In the meantime all those lives stunted for lack of opportunity seem a mere spectacle; they fail to move us.

On the Financial Crisis

The current financial crisis can make us overlook the fact that it originated in a profound human crisis: the denial of the primacy of the human person! We have created new idols. The worship of the ancient golden calf has returned in a new and ruthless guise in the idolatry of money and the dictatorship of an impersonal economy lacking a truly human purpose. The worldwide crisis affecting finance and the economy lays bare their imbalances and, above all, their lack of real concern for human beings; man is reduced to one of his needs alone: consumption.

Some Thoughts from Pope Francis

On the Wealth Gap

While the earnings of a minority are growing exponentially, so too is the gap separating the majority from the prosperity enjoyed by those happy few. This imbalance is the result of ideologies which defend the absolute autonomy of the marketplace and financial speculation. Consequently, they reject the right of states, charged with vigilance for the common good, to exercise any form of control. A new tyranny is thus born, invisible and often virtual, which unilaterally and relentlessly imposes its own laws and rules. Debt and the accumulation of interest also make it difficult for countries to realize the potential of their own economies and keep citizens from enjoying their real purchasing power. To all this we can add widespread corruption and self-serving tax evasion, which have taken on worldwide dimensions. The thirst for power and possessions knows no limits. In this system, which tends to devour everything which stands in the way of increased profits, whatever is fragile, like the environment, is defenseless before the interests of a deified market, which become the only rule.

On Ethics

Behind this attitude [of a deified market] lurks a rejection of ethics and a rejection of God. Ethics has come to be viewed with a certain scornful derision. It is seen as counterproductive, too human, because it makes money and power relative. It is felt to be a threat, since it condemns the manipulation and debasement of the person. In effect, ethics leads to a God who calls for a committed response which is outside the categories of the marketplace. When these latter are absolutized, God can only be seen as uncontrollable, unmanageable, even dangerous, since he calls human beings to their full realization and to freedom from all forms of enslavement. Ethics – a non-ideological ethics – would make it possible to bring about balance and a more humane social order. With this in mind, I encourage financial experts and political leaders to ponder the words of one of the sages of antiquity [Saint John Chrysostom]: "Not to share one's wealth with the poor is to steal from them and to take away their livelihood. It is not our own goods which we hold, but theirs."

On Inequality

Today's economic mechanisms promote inordinate consumption, yet it is evident that unbridled consumerism combined with inequality proves doubly damaging to the social fabric. Inequality eventually engenders a violence which recourse to arms cannot and never will be able to resolve. It serves only to offer false hopes to those clamoring for heightened security, even though nowadays we know that weapons and violence, rather than providing solutions, create new and more serious conflicts. Some simply content themselves with blaming the poor and the poorer countries themselves for their troubles; indulging in unwarranted generalizations, they claim that the solution is an "education" that would tranquilize them, making them tame and harmless. All this becomes even more exasperating for the marginalized in the light of the widespread and deeply rooted corruption found in many countries – in their governments, businesses and institutions – whatever the political ideology of their leaders.

On Religious Freedom

We also evangelize when we attempt to confront the various challenges which can arise. On occasion these may take the form of veritable attacks on religious freedom or new persecutions directed against Christians; in some countries these have reached alarming levels of hatred and violence. In many places, the problem is more that of widespread indifference and relativism, linked to disillusionment and the crisis of ideologies which has come about as a reaction to any-thing which might appear totalitarian. This not only harms the Church but the fabric of society as a whole. We should recognize how in a culture where each person wants to be bearer of his or her own subjective truth, it becomes difficult for citizens to devise a common plan which transcends individual gain and personal ambitions.

Some Thoughts from Pope Francis

On Superficial Culture

In the prevailing culture, priority is given to the outward, the immediate, the visible, the quick, the superficial and the provisional. What is real gives way to appearances. In many countries globalization has meant a hastened deterioration of their own cultural roots and the invasion of ways of thinking and acting proper to other cultures which are economically advanced but ethically debilitated. This fact has been brought up by bishops from various continents in different Synods. The African bishops, for example, taking up the Encyclical *Sollicitudo Rei Socialis*, pointed out years ago that there have been frequent attempts to make the African countries "parts of a machine, cogs on a gigantic wheel. This is often true also in the field of social communications which, being run by centres mostly in the northern hemisphere, do not always give due consideration to the priorities and problems of such countries or respect their cultural make-up." By the same token, the bishops of Asia "underlined the external influences being brought to bear on Asian cultures. New patterns of behaviour are emerging as a result of over-exposure to the mass media... As a result, the negative aspects of the media and entertainment industries are threatening traditional values, and in particular the sacredness of marriage and the stability of the family." (John Paul II, Apostolic Exhortation Ecclesia in Asia).)

On the Rejection of the Transcendent

The process of secularization tends to reduce the faith and the Church to the sphere of the private and personal. Furthermore, by completely rejecting the transcendent, it has produced a growing deterioration of ethics, a weakening of the sense of personal and collective sin, and a steady increase in relativism. These have led to a general sense of disorientation, especially in the periods of adolescence and young adulthood which are so vulnerable to change. As the bishops of the United States of America have rightly pointed out, while the Church insists on the existence of objective moral norms which are valid for everyone, "there are those in our culture who portray this teaching as unjust, that is, as opposed to basic human rights. Such claims usually follow from a form of moral relativism that is joined, not without inconsistency, to a belief in the absolute rights of individuals. In this view, the Church is perceived as promoting a particular prejudice and as interfering with individual freedom." (United States Conference Of Catholic Bishops, Ministry to Persons with a Homosexual Inclination: Guidelines for Pastoral Care) We are living in an information-driven society which bombards us indiscriminately with data – all treated as being of equal importance – and which leads to remarkable superficiality in the area of moral discernment. In response, we need to provide an education which teaches critical thinking and encourages the development of mature moral values.

Some Thoughts from Pope Francis

On The Cultural Crisis within Families

The family is experiencing a profound cultural crisis, as are all communities and social bonds. In the case of the family, the weakening of these bonds is particularly serious because the family is the fundamental cell of society, where we learn to live with others despite our differences and to belong to one another; it is also the place where parents pass on the faith to their children. Marriage now tends to be viewed as a form of mere emotional satisfaction that can be constructed in any way or modified at will. But the indispensable contribution of marriage to society transcends the feelings and momentary needs of the couple. As the French bishops have taught, it is not born "of loving sentiment, ephemeral by definition, but from the depth of the obligation assumed by the spouses who accept to enter a total communion of life." (Conférence Des Évêques De France, Conseil Famille et Société, Élargir le mariage aux personnes de même sexe? Ouvrons le débat!)

On Urban Crime

We cannot ignore the fact that in cities human trafficking, the narcotics trade, the abuse and exploitation of minors, the abandonment of the elderly and infirm, and various forms of corruption and criminal activity take place. At the same time, what could be significant places of encounter and solidarity often become places of isolation and mutual distrust.

Some Thoughts from Pope Francis

On Christian Service

The pain and the shame we feel at the sins of some members of the Church, and at our own, must never make us forget how many Christians are giving their lives in love. They help so many people to be healed or to die in peace in makeshift hospitals. They are present to those enslaved by different addictions in the poorest places on earth. They devote themselves to the education of children and young people. They take care of the elderly who have been forgotten by everyone else. They look for ways to communicate values in hostile environments. They are dedicated in many other ways to showing an immense love for humanity inspired by the God who became man. I am grateful for the beautiful example given to me by so many Christians who joyfully sacrifice their lives and their time. This witness comforts and sustains me in my own effort to overcome selfishness and to give more fully of myself.

On Liberation Communication

Today, when the networks and means of human communication have made unprecedented advances, we sense the challenge of finding and sharing a "mystique" of living together, of mingling and encounter, of embracing and supporting one another, of stepping into this flood tide which, while chaotic, can become a genuine experience of fraternity, a caravan of solidarity, a sacred pilgrimage. Greater possibilities for communication thus turn into greater possibilities for encounter and solidarity for everyone. If we were able to take this route, it would be so good, so soothing, so liberating and hope-filled! To go out of ourselves and to join others is healthy for us. To be self-enclosed is to taste the bitter poison of immanence, and humanity will be worse for every selfish choice we make.

Some Thoughts from Pope Francis

On the Quest for Spirituality

Isolation, which is a version of immanentism, can find expression in a false autonomy which has no place for God. But in the realm of religion it can also take the form of a spiritual consumerism tailored to one's own unhealthy individualism. The return to the sacred and the quest for spirituality which mark our own time are ambiguous phenomena. Today, our challenge is not so much atheism as the need to respond adequately to many people's thirst for God, lest they try to satisfy it with alienating solutions or with a disembodied Jesus who demands nothing of us with regard to others. Unless these people find in the Church a spirituality which can offer healing and liberation, and fill them with life and peace, while at the same time summoning them to fraternal communion and missionary fruitfulness, they will end up by being taken in by solutions which neither make life truly human nor give glory to God.

On Talk

Dialogue is much more than the communication of a truth. It arises from the enjoyment of speaking and it enriches those who express their love for one another through the medium of words. This is an enrichment which does not consist in objects but in persons who share themselves in dialogue.

Some Thoughts from Pope Francis

On the Liberation and Promotion of the Poor

Each individual Christian and every community is called to be an instrument of God for the liberation and promotion of the poor, and for enabling them to be fully a part of society. This demands that we be docile and attentive to the cry of the poor and to come to their aid. A mere glance at the Scriptures is enough to make us see how our gracious Father wants to hear the cry of the poor: "I have observed the misery of my people who are in Egypt; I have heard their cry on account of their taskmasters. Indeed, I know their sufferings, and I have come down to deliver them... so I will send you..." (Ex 3:7-8, 10).

We also see how he is concerned for their needs: "When the Israelites cried out to the Lord, the Lord raised up for them a deliverer" (Jg 3:15). If we, who are God's means of hearing the poor, turn deaf ears to this plea, we oppose the Father's will and his plan; that poor person "might cry to the Lord against you, and you would incur guilt" (Dt 15:9). A lack of solidarity towards his or her needs will directly affect our relationship with God: "For if in bitterness of soul he calls down a curse upon you, his Creator will hear his prayer" (Sir 4:6). The old question always returns: "How does God's love abide in anyone who has the world's goods, and sees a brother or sister in need and yet refuses help?"

et us recall also how bluntly the apostle James speaks of the cry of the oppressed: "The wages of the laborers who mowed your fields, which you kept back by fraud, cry out, and the cries of the harvesters have reached the ears of the Lord of hosts."

On the Social Function of Property

Solidarity is a spontaneous reaction by those who recognize that the social function of property and the universal destination of goods are realities which come before private property. The private ownership of goods is justified by the need to protect and increase them, so that they can better serve the common good; for this reason, solidarity must be lived as the decision to restore to the poor what belongs to them. These convictions and habits of solidarity, when they are put into practice, open the way to other structural transformations and make them possible. Changing structures without generating new convictions and attitudes will only ensure that those same structures will become, sooner or later, corrupt, oppressive and ineffectual.

Some Thoughts from Pope Francis

On the Rights of All Peoples

Sometimes it is a matter of hearing the cry of entire peoples, the poorest peoples of the earth, since "peace is founded not only on respect for human rights, but also on respect for the rights of peoples." (Pontifical Council for Justice and Peace, Compendium of the Social Doctrine of the Church) Sadly, even human rights can be used as a justification for an inordinate defense of individual rights or the rights of the richer peoples. With due respect for the autonomy and culture of every nation, we must never forget that the planet belongs to all mankind and is meant for all mankind; the mere fact that some people are born in places with fewer resources or less development does not justify the fact that they are living with less dignity. It must be reiterated that "the more fortunate should renounce some of their rights so as to place their goods more generously at the service of others." (Paul VI, Apostolic Letter *Octogesima Adveniens*) To speak properly of our own rights, we need to broaden our perspective and to hear the plea of other peoples and other regions than those of our own country. We need to grow in a solidarity which "would allow all peoples to become the artisans of their destiny," since "every person is called to self-fulfilment." (Paul VI, Encyclical Letter *Populorum Progressio*)

On Labor Disparity

One of the aspects of today's economic system is the exploitation of the international disparity in labour costs, which weighs on thousands of people who live on less than two dollars a day. This imbalance not only fails to respect the dignity of those who provide low-cost labour, but it destroys the sources of employment in those regions in which it is the most protected. This raises the issue of creating mechanisms for the protection of the right to employment, as well as of the environment, in the presence of a growing consumerist ideology, which does not show responsibility in conflicts with cities and with Creation.

Some Thoughts from Pope Francis

On the Elderly

Homes for the elderly should be the "lungs" of humanity in a town, a neighborhood or a parish. They should be the "sanctuaries" of humanity where one who is old and weak is cared for and protected like a big brother or sister. It is so good to go visit an elderly person! Look at our children: sometimes we see them listless and sad; they go visit an elderly person and become joyful!However, the reality is that elderly people are being abandoned: the elderly are so often discarded with an attitude of abandonment, which is actually real and hidden euthanasia! It is the result of a throw away culture which is so harmful to our world. Children are thrown away, young people are thrown away, because they have no work, and the elderly are thrown away with the pretense of maintaining a "balanced" economy, which has at its centre not the human person but money. We are all called to oppose this poisonous, throw away culture!

On Religious Freedom

Authentic religion is a source of peace and not of violence! No one must use the name of God to commit violence! To kill in the name of God is a grave sacrilege. To discriminate in the name of God is inhuman.Seen in this light, religious freedom is not a right which can be guaranteed solely by existing legislation, although laws are necessary. Rather religious freedom is a shared space – like this one – an atmosphere of respect and cooperation that must be built with everyone's participation, even those who have no religious convictions.

Some Thoughts from Pope Francis

On Attitudes for Religious Freedom

Allow me to outline two attitudes which can be especially helpful in the advancement of this fundamental freedom. The first attitude is that of regarding every man and woman, even those of different religious traditions, not as rivals, less still enemies, but rather as brothers and sisters. When a person is secure of his or her own beliefs, there is no need to impose or put pressure on others: there is a conviction that truth has its own power of attraction. Deep down, we are all pilgrims on this earth, and on this pilgrim journey, as we yearn for truth and eternity, we do not live autonomous and self-sufficient individual lives; the same applies to religious, cultural and national communities. We need each other, and are entrusted to each other's care. Each religious tradition, from within, must be able to take account of others. The second attitude which fosters the promotion of religious freedom is the work done in service of the common good. Whenever adherence to a specific religious tradition gives birth to service that shows conviction, generosity and concern for the whole of society without making distinctions, then there too exists an authentic and mature living out of religious freedom. This presents itself not only as a space in which to legitimately defend one's autonomy, but also as a potential that enriches the human family as it advances. The more men and women are at the service of others, the greater their freedom!

On Remedying the Causes of Poverty

The need to resolve the structural causes of poverty cannot be delayed, not only for the pragmatic reason of its urgency for the good order of society, but because society needs to be cured of a sickness which is weakening and frustrating it, and which can only lead to new crises. Welfare projects, which meet certain urgent needs, should be considered merely temporary responses. As long as the problems of the poor are not radically resolved by rejecting the absolute autonomy of markets and financial speculation and by attacking the structural causes of inequality, no solution will be found for the world's problems or, for that matter, to any problems. Inequality is the root of social ills.

On Irksome Discourse

The dignity of each human person and the pursuit of the common good are concerns which ought to shape all economic policies. At times, however, they seem to be a mere addendum imported from without in order to fill out a political discourse lacking in perspectives or plans for true and integral development. How many words prove irksome to this system! It is irksome when the question of ethics is raised, when global solidarity is invoked, when the distribution of goods is mentioned, when reference in made to protecting labour and defending the dignity of the powerless, when allusion is made to a God who demands a commitment to justice. At other times these issues are exploited by a rhetoric which cheapens them. Casual indifference in the face of such questions empties our lives and our words of all meaning. Business is a vocation, and a noble vocation, provided that those engaged in it see themselves challenged by a greater meaning in life; this will enable them truly to serve the common good by striving to increase the goods of this world and to make them more accessible to all.

Be Revolutionary

On Market Forces

We can no longer trust in the unseen forces and the invisible hand of the market. Growth in justice requires more than economic growth, while presupposing such growth: it requires decisions, programes, mechanisms and processes specifically geared to a better distribution of income, the creation of sources of employment and an integral promotion of the poor which goes beyond a simple welfare mentality. I am far from proposing an irresponsible populism, but the economy can no longer turn to remedies that are a new poison, such as attempting to increase profits by reducing the work force and thereby adding to the ranks of the excluded.

Some Thoughts from Pope Francis

On Politicians

I ask God to give us more politicians capable of sincere and effective dialogue aimed at healing the deepest roots – and not simply the appearances – of the evils in our world! Politics, though often denigrated, remains a lofty vocation and one of the highest forms of charity, inasmuch as it seeks the common good.

On Global Economics

Economy, as the very word indicates, should be the art of achieving a fitting management of our common home, which is the world as a whole. Each meaningful economic decision made in one part of the world has repercussions everywhere else; consequently, no government can act without regard for shared responsibility. Indeed, it is becoming increasingly difficult to find local solutions for enormous global problems which overwhelm local politics with difficulties to resolve. If we really want to achieve a healthy world economy, what is needed at this juncture of history is a more efficient way of interacting which, with due regard for the sovereignty of each nation, ensures the economic well-being of all countries, not just of a few.

Some Thoughts from Pope Francis

On Papal Interest

If anyone feels offended by my words, I would respond that I speak them with affection and with the best of intentions, quite apart from any personal interest or political ideology. My words are not those of a foe or an opponent. I am interested only in helping those who are in thrall to an individualistic, indifferent and self-centered mentality to be freed from those unworthy chains and to attain a way of living and thinking which is more humane, noble and fruitful, and which will bring dignity to their presence on this earth.

On the Defense of Species

There are other weak and defenseless beings who are frequently at the mercy of economic interests or indiscriminate exploitation. I am speaking of creation as a whole. We human beings are not only the beneficiaries but also the stewards of other creatures. Thanks to our bodies, God has joined us so closely to the world around us that we can feel the desertification of the soil almost as a physical ailment, and the extinction of a species as a painful disfigurement. Let us not leave in our wake a swath of destruction and death which will affect our own lives and those of future generations.

Some Thoughts from Pope Francis

On the Nature of Peace

Peace in society cannot be understood as pacification or the mere absence of violence resulting from the domination of one part of society over others. Nor does true peace act as a pretext for justifying a social structure which silences or appeases the poor, so that the more affluent can placidly support their lifestyle while others have to make do as they can. Demands involving the distribution of wealth, concern for the poor and human rights cannot be suppressed under the guise of creating a consensus on paper or a transient peace for a contented minority. The dignity of the human person and the common good rank higher than the comfort of those who refuse to renounce their privileges. When these values are threatened, a prophetic voice must be raised.Nor is peace "simply the absence of warfare, based on a precarious balance of power; it is fashioned by efforts directed day after day towards the establishment of the ordered universe willed by God, with a more perfect justice among men." (Paul VI, Encyclical Letter *Populorum Progressio*, March 26, 1967) In the end, a peace which is not the result of integral development will be doomed; it will always spawn new conflicts and various forms of violence.

On Time and Space

A constant tension exists between fullness and limitation. Fullness evokes the desire for complete possession, while limitation is a wall set before us. Broadly speaking, "time" has to do with fullness as an expression of the horizon which constantly opens before us, while each individual moment has to do with limitation as an expression of enclosure. People live poised between each individual moment and the greater, brighter horizon of the utopian future as the final cause which draws us to itself. Here we see a first principle for progress in building a people: time is greater than space. This principle enables us to work slowly but surely, without being obsessed with immediate results. It helps us patiently to endure difficult and adverse situations, or inevitable changes in our plans. It invites us to accept the tension between fullness and limitation, and to give a priority to time.

Some Thoughts from Pope Francis

On Ideas and Realities

There also exists a constant tension between ideas and realities. Realities simply are, whereas ideas are worked out. There has to be continuous dialogue between the two, lest ideas become detached from realities. It is dangerous to dwell in the realm of words alone, of images and rhetoric. So a third principle comes into play: realities are greater than ideas. This calls for rejecting the various means of masking reality: angelic forms of purity, dictatorships of relativism, empty rhetoric, objectives more ideal than real, brands of ahistorical fundamentalism, ethical systems bereft of kindness, intellectual discourse bereft of wisdom.

On Globalization and Localization

An innate tension also exists between globalization and localization. We need to pay attention to the global so as to avoid narrowness and banality. Yet we also need to look to the local, which keeps our feet on the ground. Together, the two prevent us from falling into one of two extremes. In the first, people get caught up in an abstract, globalized universe, falling into step behind everyone else, admiring the glitter of other people's world, gaping and applauding at all the right times. At the other extreme, they turn into a museum of local folklore, a world apart, doomed to doing the same things over and over, and incapable of being challenged by novelty or appreciating the beauty which God bestows beyond their borders.

Some Thoughts from Pope Francis

On Relations with Islam

Our relationship with the followers of Islam has taken on great importance, since they are now significantly present in many traditionally Christian countries, where they can freely worship and become fully a part of society. We must never forget that they "profess to hold the faith of Abraham, and together with us they adore the one, merciful God, who will judge humanity on the last day." The sacred writings of Islam have retained some Christian teachings; Jesus and Mary receive profound veneration and it is admirable to see how Muslims both young and old, men and women, make time for daily prayer and faithfully take part in religious services. Many of them also have a deep conviction that their life, in its entirety, is from God and for God. They also acknowledge the need to respond to God with an ethical commitment and with mercy towards those most in need.

Be Revolutionary

On Embracing Muslims

In order to sustain dialogue with Islam, suitable training is essential for all involved, not only so that they can be solidly and joyfully grounded in their own identity, but so that they can also acknowledge the values of others, appreciate the concerns underlying their demands and shed light on shared beliefs. We Christians should embrace with affection and respect Muslim immigrants to our countries in the same way that we hope and ask to be received and respected in countries of Islamic tradition. I ask and I humbly entreat those countries to grant Christians freedom to worship and to practice their faith, in light of the freedom which followers of Islam enjoy in Western countries! Faced with disconcerting episodes of violent fundamentalism, our respect for true followers of Islam should lead us to avoid hateful generalizations, for authentic Islam and the proper reading of the Koran are opposed to every form of violence.

Some Thoughts from Pope Francis

On Mary

Mary was able to turn a stable into a home for Jesus, with poor swaddling clothes and an abundance of love. She is the handmaid of the Father who sings his praises. She is the friend who is ever concerned that wine not be lacking in our lives. She is the woman whose heart was pierced by a sword and who understands all our pain. As mother of all, she is a sign of hope for peoples suffering the birth pangs of justice. She is the missionary who draws near to us and accompanies us throughout life, opening our hearts to faith by her maternal love. As a true mother, she walks at our side, she shares our struggles and she constantly surrounds us with God's love.

On Fear of Freedom

What is our lifestyle? Do we live as children or as slaves? Do we live as people baptized in Christ, anointed by the Spirit, delivered and free? Or do we live according to the corrupt, worldly logic, doing what the devil makes us believe is in our interests? In our existential journey there is always a tendency to resist liberation; we are afraid of freedom and, paradoxically and somewhat unwittingly, we prefer slavery. Freedom frightens us because it causes us to confront time and to face our responsibility to live it well. Instead, slavery reduces time to a "moment" and thus we feel more secure, that is, it makes us live moments disconnected from their past and from our future. In other words, slavery impedes us from truly and fully living the present, because it empties it of the past and closes it to the future, to eternity. Slavery makes us believe that we cannot dream, fly, hope.

Some Thoughts from Pope Francis

On Migrants and Refugees

It is necessary to respond to the globalization of migration with the globalization of charity and cooperation, in such a way as to make the conditions of migrants more humane. At the same time, greater efforts are needed to guarantee the easing of conditions, often brought about by war or famine, which compel whole peoples to leave their native countries.Solidarity with migrants and refugees must be accompanied by the courage and creativity necessary to develop, on a world-wide level, a more just and equitable financial and economic order, as well as an increasing commitment to peace, the indispensable condition for all authentic progress.

On Slaves

Even though the international community has adopted numerous agreements aimed at ending slavery in all its forms, and has launched various strategies to combat this phenomenon, millions of people today – children, women and men of all ages – are deprived of freedom and are forced to live in conditions akin to slavery.

I think of the many men and women laborers, including minors, subjugated in different sectors, whether formally or informally, in domestic or agricultural workplaces, or in the manufacturing or mining industry; whether in countries where labour regulations fail to comply with international norms and minimum standards, or, equally illegally, in countries which lack legal protection for workers' rights.

I think also of the living conditions of many migrants who, in their dramatic odyssey, experience hunger, are deprived of freedom, robbed of their possessions, or undergo physical and sexual abuse. In a particular way, I think of those among them who, upon arriving at their destination after a grueling journey marked by fear and insecurity, are detained in at times inhumane conditions.

I think of those among them, who for different social, political and economic reasons, are forced to live clandestinely.

My thoughts also turn to those who, in order to remain within the law, agree to disgraceful living and working conditions, especially in those cases where the laws of a nation create or permit a structural dependency of migrant workers on their employers, as, for example, when the legality of their residency is made dependent on their labour contract. Yes, I am thinking of "slave labour."

I think also of persons forced into prostitution, many of whom are minors, as well as male and female sex slaves. I think of women forced into marriage, those sold for arranged marriages and those bequeathed to relatives of their deceased husbands, without any right to give or withhold their consent.

Nor can I fail to think of all those persons, minors and adults alike, who are made objects of trafficking for the sale of organs, for recruitment as soldiers, for begging, for illegal activities such as the production and sale of narcotics, or for disguised forms of cross-border adoption.

Finally, I think of all those kidnapped and held captive by terrorist groups, subjected to their purposes as combatants, or, above all in the case of young girls and women, to be used as sex slaves. Many of these disappear, while others are sold several times over, tortured, mutilated or killed.

Be Revolutionary

On the Causes of Slavery

Today, as in the past, slavery is rooted in a notion of the human person which allows him or her to be treated as an object. Whenever sin corrupts the human heart and distances us from our Creator and our neighbours, the latter are no longer regarded as beings of equal dignity, as brothers or sisters sharing a common humanity, but rather as objects. Whether by coercion or deception, or by physical or psychological duress, human persons created in the image and likeness of God are deprived of their freedom, sold and reduced to being the property of others. They are treated as means to an end.

Alongside this deeper cause – the rejection of another person's humanity – there are other causes which help to explain contemporary forms of slavery.

Among these, I think in the first place of poverty, underdevelopment and exclusion, especially when combined with a lack of access to education or scarce, even non-existent, employment opportunities.

Not infrequently, the victims of human trafficking and slavery are people who look for a way out of a situation of extreme poverty; taken in by false promises of employment, they often end up in the hands of criminal networks which organize human trafficking. These networks are skilled in using modern means of communication as a way of luring young men and women in various parts of the world.

Another cause of slavery is corruption on the part of people willing to do anything for financial gain. Slave labour and human trafficking often require the complicity of intermediaries, be they law enforcement personnel, state officials, or civil and military institutions. "This occurs when money, and not the human person, is at the centre of an economic system. Yes, the person, made in the image of God and charged with dominion over all creation, must be at the centre of every social or economic system. When the person is replaced by mammon, a subversion of values occurs." (Address to Participants in the World Meeting of Popular Movements, October 28, 2014)

Further causes of slavery include armed conflicts, violence, criminal activity and terrorism. Many people are kidnapped in order to be sold, enlisted as combatants, or sexually exploited, while others are forced to emigrate, leaving everything behind: their country, home, property, and even members of their family. They are driven to seek an alternative to these terrible conditions even at the risk of their personal dignity and their very lives; they risk being drawn into that vicious circle which makes them prey to misery, corruption and their baneful consequences.

On the Seeking of Truth

Every human being is a "seeker" of the truth of his own origin and of his own destiny. In the person's mind and in the "heart," thoughts and questions arise, which cannot be repressed or smothered, such that they emerge from a profound place and are intrinsic to one's intimate essence. They are questions of religion and, in order to fully manifest themselves, require religious freedom. They seek to shed light on the authentic meaning of existence, on the links that bind it to the cosmos and to history, and seek to rend the darkness that would engulf human history should such questions not be asked, should they remain unanswered.

Some Thoughts from Pope Francis

On Religious Freedom

Reason recognizes in religious freedom a fundamental human right which reflects the highest human dignity, the ability to seek the truth and conform to it, and recognizes in it a condition which is indispensable to the ability to deploy all of one's own potentiality. Religious freedom is not only that of private thought or worship. It is the liberty to live, both privately and publicly, according to the ethical principals resulting from found truth. This is a great challenge in the globalized world, where weak thought — which is like a disease — also lowers the general ethical level, and in the name of a false concept of tolerance, it ends in persecuting those who defend the truth about man and its ethical consequences.

Be Revolutionary

On Financial Markets

It is important that ethics once again play its due part in the world of finance and that markets serve the interests of peoples and the common good of humanity. It is increasingly intolerable that financial markets are shaping the destiny of peoples rather than serving their needs, or that the few derive immense wealth from financial speculation while the many are deeply burdened by the consequences.

Some Thoughts from Pope Francis

On Legacy

Our world is a legacy bequeathed to us from past generations, but it is also on loan to us from our children: our children who are weary, worn out by conflicts and yearning for the dawn of peace, our children who plead with us to tear down the walls of enmity and to set out on the path of dialogue and peace, so that love and friendship will prevail.Many, all too many, of those children have been innocent victims of war and violence, saplings cut down at the height of their promise. It is our duty to ensure that their sacrifice is not in vain. The memory of these children instils in us the courage of peace, the strength to persevere undaunted in dialogue, the patience to weave, day by day, an ever more robust fabric of respectful and peaceful coexistence, for the glory of God and the good of all.

Be Revolutionary

On the Courage to Make Peace

Peacemaking calls for courage, much more so than warfare. It calls for the courage to say yes to encounter and no to conflict: yes to dialogue and no to violence; yes to negotiations and no to hostilities; yes to respect for agreements and no to acts of provocation; yes to sincerity and no to duplicity. All of this takes courage, it takes strength and tenacity.

Some Thoughts from Pope Francis

On Expectations of the G20

The whole world expects from the G20 an ever broader agreement which can lead, through the United Nations legal system, to a definitive halt to the unjust aggression directed at different religious and ethnic groups, including minorities, in the Middle East. It should also lead to eliminating the root causes of terrorism, which has reached proportions hitherto unimaginable; these include poverty, underdevelopment and exclusion. It has become more and more evident that the solution to this grave problem cannot be a purely military one, but must also focus on those who in one way or another encourage terrorist groups through political support, the illegal oil trade or the provision of arms and technology. There is also a need for education and a heightened awareness that religion may not be exploited as a means of justifying violence.

On ISIS

The violent attacks that are sweeping across Northern Iraq cannot but awaken the consciences of all men and women of goodwill to concrete acts of solidarity by protecting those affected or threatened by violence and assuring the necessary and urgent assistance for the many displaced people as well as their safe return to their cities and their homes. The tragic experiences of the Twentieth Century, and the most basic understanding of human dignity, compels the international community, particularly through the norms and mechanisms of international law, to do all that it can to stop and to prevent further systematic violence against ethnic and religious minorities.

Some Thoughts from Pope Francis

On Global Warming

The consequences of environmental changes, which are already being dramatically felt in many countries, especially the insular states of the Pacific, remind us of the gravity of neglect and inaction. The time to find global solutions is running out. We can find appropriate solutions only if we act together and in agreement. There is therefore a clear, definitive and urgent ethical imperative to act. An effective fight against global warming will be possible only through a responsible collective action, which overcomes particular interests and behaviors and develops unfettered by political and economic pressures. A collective response which is also capable of overcoming mistrust and of fostering a culture of solidarity, of encounter and of dialogue; capable of demonstrating responsibility to protect the planet and the human family.

On Dialogue with Other Religions

When we approach a person who professes his religion with conviction, his testimony and thoughts ask us and lead us to question our own spirituality. Dialogue, thus, begins with encounter. The first knowledge of the other is born from it. Indeed, if one begins from the premise of the common affiliation inhuman nature, one can go beyond prejudices and fallacies and begin to understand the other according to a new perspective.

Some Thoughts from Pope Francis

On Grandparents

Children and young people, are the fruit of the tree that is the family: you are good fruit when the tree has deep roots — your grandparents — and a strong trunk — your parents. Jesus said that every sound tree bears good fruit but every bad tree bears evil fruit. The great human family is like a forest, where sound trees bear solidarity, communion, trust, support, security, happy sobriety, friendship. The presence of large families is a hope for society. And this is why the presence of grandparents is very important: a precious presence both for practical help, and above all for their educational contribution. Grandparents preserve in themselves the values of a people, of a family, and they help parents pass them on to the children. In the last century, in many European countries, it was the grandparents who passed on the faith: they secretly took the child to receive Baptism and passed on the faith.

On the Olympics

The Olympic motto — "Citius, altius, fortius" — is not an incitement to the supremacy of one nation over another, of one people over another, or even of the exclusion of the weakest and least protected. But it represents the challenge to which we are all called, not only the athletes: that of taking on the toil, the sacrifice, to reach life's important goals, accepting one's limitations without allowing oneself to be impeded by them but striving to excel.

Some Thoughts from Pope Francis

On Hidden Slavery

Despite the great efforts of many, modern slavery continues to be an atrocious scourge that is present throughout the world on a broad scale, even as tourism. This crime of "lèse-humanity" masquerades behind seemingly acceptable customs, but in reality claims its victims through prostitution, human trafficking, forced labour, slave labour, mutilation, the sale of organs, the consumption of drugs and child labour. It hides behind closed doors, in particular places, in the streets, automobiles, factories, the countryside, in fishing boats and many other places. And this happens both in towns and villages, in the reception centres of the wealthiest nations as well as in those of the poorest. And the worst thing is that this situation, unfortunately, grows more serious every day.

On Islamophobia

On Islamophobia: It's true that there has been a reaction to these acts of terrorism, not just in this region but in Africa as well: "If this is Islam it makes me angry!." So many Muslims feel offended, they say: "But that is not what we are. The Quran is a prophetic book of peace. This is not Islam." I can understand this. And I sincerely believe that we cannot say all Muslims are terrorists, just as we cannot say that all Christians are fundamentalists – we also have fundamentalists among us, all religions have these small groups.

I told [Turkish] President [Erdogan] that it would be good to issue a clear condemnation against these kinds of groups. All religious leaders, scholars, clerics, intellectuals and politicians should do this. This way they hear it from their leaders' mouth. There needs to be international condemnation from Muslims across the world. It must be said, "No, this is not what the Quran is about!" This is the first thing.

Getting back to [Islamophobia and Christianophobia, there should always be a distinction between what a religion proposes and the concrete practice of that proposal by any specific government. One may say: "I'm Muslim" – "I'm Jewish" – "I'm Christian." But you govern your country not as Muslim or Jewish or Christian. There's an abyss. The distinction must be made, because so often the name is used but the reality does not reflect what the religion says.

Some Thoughts from Pope Francis

On Christianophobia

On Christianophobia: It's true, I'm not going to soften my words, no. We Christians are being chased out of the Middle East. In some cases, as we have seen in Iraq, in the Mosul area, they have to leave or pay a tax which then makes no sense. And other times they push us out wearing white gloves. For example, in one country, a husband lives in one place and his wife in another.... No, let the man come and live with his wife. No, no: let the woman leave, and leave the house free. This is happening in several countries. It's as if they wished that there were no more Christians, that nothing remain of Christianity. In that region this is happening. It's true, it's first of all a result of terrorism, but when it's done diplomatically with white gloves, it's because there's something behind it. This is not good.

On His Prayer in a Mosque

I went to Turkey as a pilgrim, not a tourist. And I went especially for today's feast. I went precisely in order to celebrate it with Patriarch Bartholomew. It was for a religious reason. But then, when I entered the Mosque, I couldn't say: now, I'm a tourist! No, it was completely religious. And I saw that wonder! The Mufti explained things very well to me, with such meekness, and using the Quran, which speaks of Mary and John the Baptist. He explained it all to me.... At that moment I felt the need to pray. So I asked him: "Shall we pray a little?" To which he responded: "Yes, yes." I prayed for Turkey, for peace, for the Mufti, for everyone and for myself, as I need it … I prayed, sincerely…. Most of all, I prayed for peace, and I said: "Lord, let's put an end to these wars!" Thus, it was a moment of sincere prayer.

Some Thoughts from Pope Francis

On the Ongoing Third World War

I am convinced that we are experiencing a Third World War [fought] piecemeal, a war in chapters, everywhere. There are rivalries, political problems and economic problems and commercial ones, and not just these, but many more that are directed to keeping alive this system where the god of money is at the centre instead of the human person. Arms trafficking is terrible; it is one of the most powerful businesses right now. Therefore I believe that this reality is increasing because arms are being distributed. I remember that in September of last year, there was talk that Syria possessed chemical weapons: I do not believe Syria is in a position to produce chemical weapons. Who sold them these? Perhaps those who accused them of having them in the first place? I don't know. There is a great mystery surrounding this weapons business.

On Atomic Weapons

The example of Hiroshima and Nagasaki: Humanity has not learnt its lesson, they haven't learned. They are incapable of learning the basic concept of this issue. God gave us creation so that we could create culture out of this primordial lack of culture. We can advance it. Humans did this and discovered nuclear energy which has many positive uses, but they also used it to destroy creation, humanity. This became a second kind of lack of culture: that primordial lack of culture which man needed to transform into culture becomes another lack of culture, a second one. And this lack of culture, I don't want to say the end of the world, but it is a "terminal" culture. Then we will need to start from the beginning, and it is terrible how your [Japanese] cities had to start from the beginning again.

Some Thoughts from Pope Francis

On Middle East Peace

Muslim, Jewish and Christian – both in the provision and practice of the law, enjoy the same rights and respect the same duties. They will then find it easier to see each other as brothers and sisters who are travelling the same path, seeking always to reject misunderstandings while promoting cooperation and concord. Freedom of religion and freedom of expression, when truly guaranteed to each person, will help friendship to flourish and thus become an eloquent sign of peace. The Middle East, Europe and the world all await this maturing of friendship. The Middle East, in particular, has for too long been a theatre of fratricidal wars, one born of the other, as if the only possible response to war and violence must be new wars and further acts of violence. How much longer must the Middle East suffer the consequences of this lack of peace? We must not resign ourselves to ongoing conflicts as if the situation can never change for the better! With the help of God, we can and we must renew the courage of peace! Such courage will lead to a just, patient and determined use of all available means of negotiation, and in this way achieve the concrete goals of peace and sustainable development.

On Hunger

Interest in the production, availability and accessibility of foodstuffs, in climate change and in agricultural trade should certainly inspire rules and technical measures, but the first concern must be the individual person, who lacks daily nourishment, who has given up thinking about life, family and social relationships, and instead fights only for survival. At the inauguration of the First Conference on Nutrition in 1992, St. Pope John Paul II warned the international community of the risk of the "paradox of abundance," in which there is food for everyone, but not everyone can eat, while waste, excessive consumption and the use of food for other purposes is visible before our very eyes. This is the paradox! Unfortunately, this "paradox" persists. There are few subjects about which there are as many fallacies as there are about hunger; few topics are as likely to be manipulated by data, statistics, by national security demands, corruption, or by grim references to the economic crisis.

Some Thoughts from Pope Francis

On Solidarity and Hunger

Subconsciously we suspect that the word solidarity should be removed from the dictionary. Our societies are characterized by growing individualism and division: this ends up depriving the weakest of a decent life, and provokes revolts against institutions. When there is a lack of solidarity in a country, the effects are felt by all. Indeed, solidarity is the attitude that enables people to reach out to others and establish mutual relations on this sense of brotherhood that overcomes differences and limits, and inspires us to seek the common good together. Human beings, as they become aware of being partly responsible for the plan of Creation, become capable of mutual respect, instead of fighting among themselves, damaging and impoverishing the planet. States, too, understood as communities of individuals and peoples, are called to act concertedly, to be willing to help each other through the principles and norms offered by international law. An inexhaustible source of inspiration, natural law, is inscribed in the human heart, and speaks to everyone in understandable terms: love, justice, peace, elements that are inseparable from each other. Like people, States and international institutions are called to welcome and nurture these values in a spirit of dialogue and mutual listening. In this way, the aim of feeding the human family becomes feasible.

On the Concept of Person

"Dignity" was a pivotal concept in the process of rebuilding which followed the Second World War. Our recent past has been marked by the concern to protect human dignity, in contrast to the manifold instances of violence and discrimination which, even in Europe, took place in the course of the centuries. Recognition of the importance of human rights came about as the result of a lengthy process, entailing much suffering and sacrifice, which helped shape an awareness of the unique worth of each individual human person. This awareness was grounded not only in historical events, but above all in European thought, characterized as it is by an enriching encounter whose "distant springs are many, coming from Greece and Rome, from Celtic, Germanic and Slavic sources, and from Christianity which profoundly shaped them," (John Paul II) thus forging the very concept of the "person."

Some Thoughts from Pope Francis

On Dignity and Economic Interests

In the end, what kind of dignity is there without the possibility of freely expressing one's thought or professing one's religious faith? What dignity can there be without a clear juridical framework which limits the rule of force and enables the rule of law to prevail over the power of tyranny? What dignity can men and women ever enjoy if they are subjected to all types of discrimination? What dignity can a person ever hope to find when he or she lacks food and the bare essentials for survival and, worse yet, when they lack the work which confers dignity?Promoting the dignity of the person means recognizing that he or she possesses inalienable rights which no one may take away arbitrarily, much less for the sake of economic interests.

Be Revolutionary

On Individual Rights and Duties

At the same time, however, care must be taken not to fall into certain errors which can arise from a misunderstanding of the concept of human rights and from its misuse. Today there is a tendency to claim ever broader individual rights – I am tempted to say individualistic; underlying this is a conception of the human person as detached from all social and anthropological contexts, as if the person were a "monad," increasingly unconcerned with other surrounding "monads."

The equally essential and complementary concept of duty no longer seems to be linked to such a concept of rights. As a result, the rights of the individual are upheld, without regard for the fact that each human being is part of a social context wherein his or her rights and duties are bound up with those of others and with the common good of society itself.

I believe, therefore, that it is vital to develop a culture of human rights which wisely links the individual, or better, the personal aspect, to that of the common good, of the "all of us" made up of individuals, families and intermediate groups who together constitute society.In fact, unless the rights of each individual are harmoniously ordered to the greater good, those rights will end up being considered limitless and consequently will become a source of conflicts and violence.

On Loneliness

In my view, one of the most common diseases in Europe today is the loneliness typical of those who have no connection with others. This is especially true of the elderly, who are often abandoned to their fate, and also in the young who lack clear points of reference and opportunities for the future. It is also seen in the many poor who dwell in our cities and in the disorientation of immigrants who came here seeking a better future.

Be Revolutionary

On Transcendence of Heaven and Earth

One of the most celebrated frescoes of Raphael is found in the Vatican and depicts the so-called "School of Athens." Plato and Aristotle are in the centre. Plato's finger is pointed upward, to the world of ideas, to the sky, to heaven as we might say. Aristotle holds his hand out before him, towards the viewer, towards the world, concrete reality. This strikes me as a very apt image of Europe and her history, made up of the constant interplay between heaven and earth, where the sky suggests that openness to the transcendent – to God – which has always distinguished the peoples of Europe, while the earth represents Europe's practical and concrete ability to confront situations and problems.

The future of Europe depends on the recovery of the vital connection between these two elements. A Europe which is no longer open to the transcendent dimension of life is a Europe which risks slowly losing its own soul and that "humanistic spirit" which it still loves and defends.

Some Thoughts from Pope Francis

On Stewardship of Nature

Our earth needs constant concern and attention. Each of us has a personal responsibility to care for creation, this precious gift which God has entrusted to us. This means, on the one hand, that nature is at our disposal, to enjoy and use properly. Yet it also means that we are not its masters. Stewards, but not masters. We need to love and respect nature, but "instead we are often guided by the pride of dominating, possessing, manipulating, exploiting; we do not 'preserve' the earth, we do not respect it, we do not consider it as a freely-given gift to look after.

Be Revolutionary

On Christians as a Soul

An anonymous second-century author wrote that "Christians are to the world what the soul is to the body."[13] The function of the soul is to support the body, to be its conscience and its historical memory. A two-thousand-year-old history links Europe and Christianity. It is a history not free of conflicts and errors, and sins, but one constantly driven by the desire to work for the good of all. We see this in the beauty of our cities, and even more in the beauty of the many works of charity and constructive human cooperation throughout this continent. This history, in large part, must still be written. It is our present and our future. It is our identity. Europe urgently needs to recover its true features in order to grow, as its founders intended, in peace and harmony, since it is not yet free of conflicts.

Some Thoughts from Pope Francis

On Experimentation with Life

We are living in a time of experimentation with life. But it is harmful experimentation. Making children, rather than accepting them as a gift, as I said. Playing with life. Be careful, because this is a sin against the Creator: against God the Creator, who created things this way. Many times in my life as a priest, I have heard objections.

"Tell me, why, for example, does the Church oppose abortion? Is it a religious problem?"

"No, no. It's not a religious problem"

"Is it a philosophical problem?"

"No, it's not a philosophical problem."

It is a scientific problem, because there is a human life there and it is not licit to eliminate a human life to resolve a problem.

"But no, the modern school of thought...."

"Listen, in the old and the modern schools of thought, the word kill means the same thing!"

The same is true for euthanasia. We all know that with so many elderly people in this throw-away culture, euthanasia is being performed in secret. There is also another. And this is saying to God: "No, I will end life, as I see fit."

On Economy and Finance

Economy and finance are dimensions of human activity and can be occasions of encounter, of dialogue, of cooperation, of recognized rights and of services rendered, of dignity affirmed in work. But in order for this it is necessary to always place man with his dignity at the centre, countering the dynamics that tend to homologize everything and place money at the apex. When money becomes the end and the motive of every activity and of every venture, then the utilitarian perspective and brute logic — which do not respect people — prevail, resulting in the widespread collapse of the values of solidarity and respect for the human being.

Some Thoughts from Pope Francis

On Religious Diversity

It is widely thought that coexistence is only possible by hiding one's own religious affiliation, by meeting in a kind of neutral space, devoid of references to transcendence. But here, too: how would it be possible to create true relationships, to build a society that is a common home, by imposing that each person set aside what he considers to be an intimate part of his very being? It is impossible to think of fraternity being "born in a laboratory." Of course it is necessary that all things be done while respecting the convictions of others, and of unbelievers, but we must have the courage and patience to come together as we are. The future lies in the respectful coexistence of diversity, not in homologation to a single theoretically neutral way of thought. Throughout history we have seen the tragedy of narrow mindedness.

Be Revolutionary

On Rugby

Rugby is a very nice sport, and I am saying this because this is how I see it: it is a tough sport, there is body contact but there is no violence, there is great loyalty and great respect. Playing rugby is tiring, **no es un paseo,** it is not a leisurely walk! And I think this is useful to temper the character, the strength of willpower. Another aspect that stands out is the balance between the group and the individual. There are the famous "scrums" that are at times shocking! The two teams engage, two compact teams push together against each other and balance each other out. And then there are individual moves, the sprints to score a try. That's it, in rugby you run towards the "goal"! Such a beautiful word, so important. It makes us think about life, because our whole life moves toward a goal; and this search — the search for the goal — is strenuous, it demands a struggle, commitment. And it is important not to run alone! In order to arrive you must run together: the ball is passed from hand to hand and you move forward together until you reach the goal. Then you celebrate!

Some Thoughts from Pope Francis

On Torture

Today, torture is an almost, I would say, ordinary means used in intelligence work, in trials... And torture is a sin against humanity, it is a crime against humanity. And to Catholics, I say: to torture a person is a mortal sin; it is a grave sin, but even more, it is a sin against humanity. Cruelty and torture. I would like it very much if you, in your media, would reflect on these things. How do you see these things today? What is the level of mankind's cruelty? What do you think about torture? I think it could benefit all of us to reflect on this.

On Stopping Aggressors

[...W]here there is an unjust aggression, I can only say that it is licit to stop the unjust aggressor. I emphasize the word: "stop." I'm not saying drop bombs, make war, but stop the aggressor. The means used to stop him would have to be evaluated. Stopping an unjust aggressor is licit. But we also need to remember! How many times, with this excuse of stopping an unjust aggressor, the powers have taken over peoples and carried on an actual war of conquest!

Some Thoughts from Pope Francis

On Diplomacy

The quest for peace represents a challenge for each of us, and in a particular way for those of you dedicated to the pursuit of the common good of the human family through the patient work of diplomacy. It is the perennial challenge of breaking down the walls of distrust and hatred by promoting a culture of reconciliation and solidarity. For diplomacy, as the art of the possible, is based on the firm and persevering conviction that peace can be won through quiet listening and dialogue, rather than by mutual recriminations, fruitless criticisms and displays of force.

On the Work of Justice

Peace is not simply the absence of war, but the work of justice. And justice, as a virtue, calls for the discipline of forbearance; it demands that we not forget past injustices but overcome them through forgiveness, tolerance and cooperation. It demands the willingness to discern and attain mutually beneficial goals, building foundations of mutual respect, understanding and reconciliation.

Some Thoughts from Pope Francis

On Cultivation

This is one of the greatest challenges of our time: changing to a form of development which seeks to respect creation. I see America — my homeland, too: many forests, stripped, which become land that cannot be cultivated, which cannot give life. This is our sin: exploiting the land and not allowing it to give us what it has within it, with our help through cultivation.

Be Revolutionary

On Playing with Children

When I go to confession and I confess — now not as often as when I was in the other diocese — when a young mom or dad comes, I ask: "How many children do you have?," and they tell me. And I ask another question, always: "Tell me: do you play with your children?." Most of them answer: "What are you asking, Father?" — "Yes, yes: do you play? Do you spend time with your children?" We are losing this capacity, this wisdom of playing with our children. The economic situation pushes us to this, to lose this. Please, spend time with our children!

Some Thoughts from Pope Francis

On Unemployment

We are in a world economic system which is centered on money, not on the human person. A genuine economic system is centered on man and woman, the human person. Today money is at the center. To maintain itself, its equilibrium, this system has to adopt certain "throwaway" measures. So you throw away children – the birth rate in Europe is not very high! . . . Children are discarded. The elderly are discarded: old people are not useful; in the present situation, at this moment, we visit them because they are retired and needy, but it is a matter of the present situation. The elderly are also discarded with situations of hidden euthanasia in many countries. In a word, they are given medical care to a certain point, and then...

And right now young people are being discarded and this is something very serious. It is extremely serious. In Italy, I believe that the rate of unemployment among the young is nearly 40%, I'm not sure. In Spain, I am sure that it is about 50%. And in Andalusia, in southern Spain, it is 60%! This means that there is an entire generation which is "neither-nor": they neither study nor work, and this is something really serious! A generation of young people is being thrown away.

On Pilgrims

A pilgrim is a person who makes himself poor and sets forth on a journey. Pilgrims set out intently toward a great and longed-for destination, and they live in the hope of a promise received. This was how Abraham lived, and this should be our spiritual attitude. We can never think ourselves self-sufficient, masters of our own lives. We cannot be content with remaining withdrawn, secure in our convictions. Before the mystery of God we are all poor. We realize that we must constantly be prepared to go out from ourselves, docile to God's call and open to the future that he wishes to create for us.In our earthly pilgrimage we are not alone. We cross paths with other faithful; at times we share with them a stretch of the road and at other times we experience with them a moment of rest which refreshes us.

On Learning

I love school because it is synonymous with openness to reality. At least it should be! Yet it does not always manage to be so, and so that means that the structure needs to be adapted a little. Going to school means opening one's mind and heart to reality, in the wealth of its aspects, of its dimensions. And we do not have the right to be afraid of reality! School teaches us to understand reality. And this is so very beautiful!Teachers are the first ones who must remain open to reality — I heard the testimony of your teachers; it pleased me to see them so open to reality — with minds still open to learning! For if a teacher is not open to learning, he or she is not a good teacher and isn't even interesting; young people understand that, they have a "nose" for it, and they are attracted by professors whose thoughts are open, "unfinished," who are seeking something "more," and thus they infect students with this attitude.

On Education

I love school because it educates us in the true, the good and the beautiful. All three go together. Education cannot be neutral. It is either positive or negative; it either enriches or impoverishes; it either makes a person develop or depresses him, it can even corrupt him. And what we heard today is so important in education: a clean defeat is always better than a dirty victory!...Thus we cultivate within ourselves the true, the good and the beautiful; and we learn that these three dimensions are never separated but rather are interwoven. If something is true, it is good and it is beautiful; if something is beautiful, it is good and it is true; if it is good, it is true and it is beautiful. And together these elements make us grow and help us to love life, even when we are unwell, even amid difficulties. True education makes us love life, and it opens us to the fullness of life!

On Hope

Hope never disappoints. It never disappoints! A hope that moves forward. I would advise you to read often Chapter 11 of the Letter to the Hebrews, that chapter of hope. And to learn that many of our forefathers took this path and did not see the results, but they anticipated them beforehand. Hope.... This is what I wish for you. Many thanks for all you do in the Church; many thanks for your prayers and work. Thanks for the hope. And do not forget: be revolutionary!

On Homosexuality

In Buenos Aires I used to receive letters from homosexual persons who are "socially wounded" because they tell me that they feel like the church has always condemned them. But the church does not want to do this. During the return flight from Rio de Janeiro I said that if a homosexual person is of good will and is in search of God, I am no one to judge. By saying this, I said what the catechism says. Religion has the right to express its opinion in the service of the people, but God in creation has set us free: it is not possible to interfere spiritually in the life of a person.

"A person once asked me, in a provocative manner, if I approved of homosexuality. I replied with another question: 'Tell me: when God looks at a gay person, does he endorse the existence of this person with love, or reject and condemn this person?' We must always consider the person.

On Soccer

As a boy I went to the stadium a number of times and I have fond memories of it. I went by myself and with my family. They were joyful moments on a Sunday spent together with my family. I would hope that football and all other popular sports can take back that element of celebration. Today football also operates within the world of business, marketing, television, etc. But the economic aspect must not prevail over that of the sport; it risks contaminating everything on the international, national, and even local level. Therefore, those at the top must react in a positive way, by restoring athletic dignity to these events.

On Healthcare

[I]n order to talk about total health, it is necessary not to lose sight of the fact that the human person, created in the image and likeness of God, is a unity of body and spirit. The Greeks were more precise: body, soul and spirit. The human person is unity. These two elements may be distinguished but not separated, because the person is one. Thus also illness, the experience of pain and suffering, involves not only the physical dimension, but man in his totality. That is why there is need for integral treatment, which considers the person as a whole and joins medical care — "technical" care — to human, psychological and social support, for the physician has to care for all aspects: the human body in its psychological, social and spiritual dimensions, as well as the spiritual accompaniment and support for the sick person's family. It is, therefore, imperative that healthcare workers be those who are "led by an integrally human view of illness and who as a result are able to effect a fully human approach to the sick person who is suffering" (John Paul II, *Dolentium Hominum*)

Some Thoughts from Pope Francis

On Right to Life

We know that human life is sacred and inviolable. Every civil right rests on the recognition of the first and fundamental right, that of life, which is not subordinate to any condition, be it quantitative, economic or, least of all, ideological. Just as the commandment 'Thou shalt not kill' sets a clear limit in order to safeguard the value of human life, today we also have to say 'thou shalt not' to an economy of exclusion and inequality. Such an economy kills.... Human beings are themselves considered consumer goods to be used and then discarded. We have created a 'throw away' culture which is now spreading. And in this way life, too, ends up being thrown away.

On Economy and Morality

One of the gravest risks our epoch faces, amid the opportunities offered by a market equipped with every technological innovation, is the divorce between economics and morality, the basic ethical norms of human nature are increasingly neglected. It is therefore necessary to express the strongest possible opposition to every direct attack on life, especially against the innocent and defenseless, and the unborn in a mother's womb is the example of innocence par excellence.

Some Thoughts from Pope Francis

On Abuse of Children by Priests

I feel compelled to personally assume all the evil which some priests — really quite a number, but not in proportion to the total number — to assume the burden myself and to ask for forgiveness for the harm they have done for having sexually abused children. The Church is aware of this damage. It is a personal, moral damage carried out by men of the Church, and we will not take one step backward concerning the treatment of this problem and the sanctions that must be imposed. On the contrary, I believe that we have to be very strong. There is no messing around when it comes to children!

On Educational Experimentation

I would like to express my rejection of any kind of educational experimentation on children. We cannot experiment on children and young people. They are not lab specimens! The horrors of the manipulation of education that we experienced in the great genocidal dictatorships of the 20th century have not disappeared; they have retained a current relevance under various guises and proposals and, with the pretense of modernity, push children and young people to walk on the dictatorial path of "only one form of thought." A little over a week ago a great teacher said to me… "At times with these projects — referring to actual educational projects — one doesn't know whether the child is going to school or to a re-education camp."

Some Thoughts from Pope Francis

On New Culture

Working for human rights presupposes the vital aim of fostering anthropological formation, of proper knowledge of the reality of the human person, and knowing how to respond to the problems and challenges posed by contemporary culture and the mentality propagated by the mass media. Obviously this does not mean we should take refuge in hidden protected areas, that today are unable to foster life, that belong to a past culture... No, not this, this is not good.... We should face the challenges the new culture launches with the positive values of the human person.

Be Revolutionary

On Human Trafficking

Human trafficking is an open wound on the body of contemporary society, a scourge upon the body of Christ. It is a crime against humanity.

On Mayors

The mayor among the people. One cannot understand a mayor who isn't found there, because he is a mediator, a mediator amid the needs of the people. And the danger is to become a mayor who is not a mediator but an 'intermediary'?. What is the difference? An intermediary exploits the needs of the parties involved and takes a piece for himself, like the owner of a small shop and one of his suppliers, and he takes a little here and a little there; such a mayor, if he exists — I am speaking hypothetically — this sort of mayor does not know what it means to be a mayor. Instead, a mediator is one who himself pays with his life for the unity of his people, for the well-being of his people, to carry forward the various solutions to the needs of his people. After time dedicated to being a mayor, this man or woman becomes tired, tired, with a desire to rest a little, but also with a heart full of love because he or she has acted as a mediator.

On His Own Happiness

I feel happy! I am happy because…I don't know why…maybe because I have a job, I'm not unemployed; I have an occupation, a job as a pastor! I am happy because I found my way in life, and following this way makes me happy. It's also a calm happiness because at this age, it isn't the happiness o a young person. There a difference. A certain interior peace, a deep peace, a happiness that even comes with age. And also with a path that always brings problems. Problems still exist, but this happiness does not fade with the problems. No. You see the problems, suffer because of them, and then go on ahead, do something to solve them and then go on ahead. But in the depth of the heart reside this peace and this happiness.

On Work

Faced with current economic developments and the distress that employment is experiencing, it is necessary to reaffirm that work is essential for society, for families and for individuals. Work, in fact, directly concerns the human person, his life, his freedom and his happiness. The primary value of work is the good of the human person since it fulfills him as such, with his inner talents and his intellectual, creative and physical abilities. Hence the scope of work is not only profit and economics; its purpose above all regards man and his dignity. Man's dignity is tied to work.

On Unemployment

What can we say before the grave problem of unemployment affecting various European countries? It is the consequence of an economic system which is no longer capable of creating work, because it has placed an idol at the centre that is called money! Therefore, the various political, social and economic entities are called to promote a different approach based on justice and solidarity. This word now risks being removed from the dictionary. Solidarity: it seems like a dirty word! No! Solidarity is important, but this system is not very fond of it, it prefers to exclude it. Such human solidarity should ensure that everyone have the possibility to carry out a dignified form of work. Work is a good for everyone and it needs to be available for everyone. Periods of grave hardship and unemployment need to be addressed with the tools of creativity and solidarity. The creativity of entrepreneurs and brave artisans who look to the future with confidence and hope. And the solidarity requires that all members of society renounce something and adopt a more sober lifestyle to help all those who are in need.

Some Thoughts from Pope Francis

On Marriage Forever

It's important to ask yourself if it is possible to love each other "forever." This is a question that must be asked: is it possible to love "forever"? Today so many people are afraid of making definitive decisions. One boy said to his bishop: "I want to become a priest, but only for ten years." He was afraid of a definitive choice. But that is a general fear that comes from our culture. To make life decisions seems impossible. Today everything changes so quickly, nothing lasts long. And this mentality leads many who are preparing for marriage to say: "we are together as long as the love lasts," and then? All the best and see you later... and so ends the marriage. But what do we mean by "love"? Is it only a feeling, a psychophysical state? Certainly, if that is it, then we cannot build on anything solid. But if, instead, love is a relationship, then it is a reality that grows, and we can also say by way of example that it is built up like a home. And a home is built together, not alone! To build something here means to foster and aid growth. Dear engaged couples, you are preparing to grow together, to build this home, to live together forever. You do not want to found it on the sand of sentiments, which come and go, but on the rock of true love, the love that comes from God. The family is born from this plan of love, it wants to grow just as a home is built, as a place of affection, of help, of hope, of support. As the love of God is stable and forever, so too should we want the love on which a family is based to be stable and forever. Please, we mustn't let ourselves be overcome by the "culture of the provisory"! Today this culture invades us all, this culture of the t he provisional. This does not work!

Be Revolutionary

On Jorge Mario Bergoglio

I do not know what might be the most fitting description.... I am a sinner. This is the most accurate definition. It is not a figure of speech, a literary genre. I am a sinner.

Some Thoughts from Pope Francis

Be Revolutionary

Some Thoughts from Pope Francis

Laudato Si

An Encyclical on Care for Our Common Home

Praised be you, my Lord, with all your creatures,
especially Sir Brother Sun,
who is the day and through whom you give us light.
And he is beautiful and radiant with great splendor;
and bears a likeness of you, Most High.
Praised be you, my Lord,
through Sister Moon and the stars,
in heaven you formed them clear and precious and beautiful.
Praised be you, my Lord,
through Brother Wind,
and through the air, cloudy and serene, and every kind of weather
through whom you give sustenance to your creatures.
Praised be you, my Lord,
through Sister Water,
who is very useful and humble and precious and chaste.
 Praised be you, my Lord, through Brother Fire,
through whom you light the night,
and he is beautiful and playful and robust and strong.

Canticle of the Creatures
Francis of Assisi

1.[1] "LAUDATO SI', mi' Signore" – "Praise be to you, my Lord". In the words of this beautiful canticle, Saint Francis of Assisi reminds us that our common home is like a sister with whom we share our life and a beautiful mother who opens her arms to embrace us. "Praise be to you, my Lord, through our Sister, Mother Earth, who sustains and governs us, and who produces various fruit with coloured flowers and herbs".[1]

2. This sister now cries out to us because of the harm we have inflicted on her by our irresponsible use and abuse of the goods with which God has endowed her. We have come to see ourselves as her lords and masters, entitled to plunder her at will. The violence present in our hearts, wounded by sin, is also reflected in the symptoms of sickness evident in the soil, in the water, in the air and in all forms of life. This is why the earth herself, burdened and laid waste, is among the most abandoned and maltreated of our poor; she "groans in travail" (Rom 8:22). We have forgotten that we ourselves are dust of the earth (cf. Gen 2:7); our very bodies are made up of her elements, we breathe her air and we receive life and refreshment from her waters.

Nothing in this world is indifferent to us.

13. The urgent challenge to protect our common home includes a concern to bring the whole human family together to seek a sustainable and integral development, for we know that things can change. The Creator does not abandon us; he never forsakes his loving plan or repents of

---

1   Numbers indicate paragraphs in the original document. Paragraphs are quoted in their entirety, with omitted paragraphs indicated (redundantly) by an extra blank line.

having created us. Humanity still has the ability to work together in building our common home. Here I want to recognize, encourage and thank all those striving in countless ways to guarantee the protection of the home which we share. Particular appreciation is owed to those who tirelessly seek to resolve the tragic effects of environmental degradation on the lives of the world's poorest. Young people demand change. They wonder how anyone can claim to be building a better future without thinking of the environmental crisis and the sufferings of the excluded.

14. I urgently appeal, then, for a new dialogue about how we are shaping the future of our planet. We need a conversation which includes everyone, since the environmental challenge we are undergoing, and its human roots, concern and affect us all. The worldwide ecological movement has already made considerable progress and led to the establishment of numerous organizations committed to raising awareness of these challenges. Regrettably, many efforts to seek concrete solutions to the environmental crisis have proved ineffective, not only because of powerful opposition but also because of a more general lack of interest. Obstructionist attitudes, even on the part of believers, can range from denial of the problem to indifference, nonchalant resignation or blind confidence in technical solutions. We require a new and universal solidarity. As the bishops of Southern Africa have stated: "Everyone's talents and involvement are needed to redress the damage caused by human abuse of God's creation."[2] All of us can cooperate as instruments of God for the care of creation, each according to his or her own culture, experience, involvements and talents.

---

[2] SOUTHERN AFRICAN CATHOLIC BISHOPS' CONFERENCE, Pastoral Statement on the Environmental Crisis (5 September 1999).

Be Revolutionary

CHAPTER ONE

What is Happening to Our Common Home

17. Theological and philosophical reflections on the situation of humanity and the world can sound tiresome and abstract, unless they are grounded in a fresh analysis of our present situation, which is in many ways unprecedented in the history of humanity. So, before considering how faith brings new incentives and requirements with regard to the world of which we are a part, I will briefly turn to what is happening to our common home.

18. The continued acceleration of changes affecting humanity and the planet is coupled today with a more intensified pace of life and work which might be called "rapidification." Although change is part of the working of complex systems, the speed with which human activity has developed contrasts with the naturally slow pace of biological evolution. Moreover, the goals of this rapid and constant change are not necessarily geared to the common good or to integral and sustainable human development. Change is something desirable, yet it becomes a source of anxiety when it causes harm to the world and to the quality of life of much of humanity.

19. Following a period of irrational confidence in progress and human abilities, some sectors of society are now adopting a more critical approach. We see increasing sensitivity to the environment and the need to protect nature, along with a growing concern, both genuine and distressing, for what is happening to our planet. Let us review, however cursorily, those questions which are troubling us today and which we can no longer sweep under the carpet. Our goal is not to amass information or to satisfy curiosity, but rather to become painfully aware, to dare to

turn what is happening to the world into our own personal suffering and thus to discover what each of us can do about it.

I. Pollution and Climate Change

Pollution, waste and the throwaway culture

20. Some forms of pollution are part of people's daily experience. Exposure to atmospheric pollutants produces a broad spectrum of health hazards, especially for the poor, and causes millions of premature deaths. People take sick, for example, from breathing high levels of smoke from fuels used in cooking or heating. There is also pollution that affects everyone, caused by transport, industrial fumes, substances which contribute to the acidification of soil and water, fertilizers, insecticides, fungicides, herbicides and agrotoxins in general. Technology, which, linked to business interests, is presented as the only way of solving these problems, in fact proves incapable of seeing the mysterious network of relations between things and so sometimes solves one problem only to create others.

21. Account must also be taken of the pollution produced by residue, including dangerous waste present in different areas. Each year hundreds of millions of tons of waste are generated, much of it non-biodegradable, highly toxic and radioactive, from homes and businesses, from construction and demolition sites, from clinical, electronic and industrial sources. The earth, our home, is beginning to look more and more like an immense pile of filth. In many parts of the planet, the elderly lament that once beautiful landscapes are now covered with rubbish. Industrial waste and chemical products utilized in cities and agricultural areas can lead to bioaccumulation in the organisms of the local population, even when levels of toxins in those places are low.

Frequently no measures are taken until after people's health has been irreversibly affected.

22. These problems are closely linked to a throwaway culture which affects the excluded just as it quickly reduces things to rubbish. To cite one example, most of the paper we produce is thrown away and not recycled. It is hard for us to accept that the way natural ecosystems work is exemplary: plants synthesize nutrients which feed herbivores; these in turn become food for carnivores, which produce significant quantities of organic waste which give rise to new generations of plants. But our industrial system, at the end of its cycle of production and consumption, has not developed the capacity to absorb and reuse waste and by-products. We have not yet managed to adopt a circular model of production capable of preserving resources for present and future generations, while limiting as much as possible the use of non-renewable resources, moderating their consumption, maximizing their efficient use, reusing and recycling them. A serious consideration of this issue would be one way of counteracting the throwaway culture which affects the entire planet, but it must be said that only limited progress has been made in this regard.

Climate as a common good

23. The climate is a common good, belonging to all and meant for all. At the global level, it is a complex system linked to many of the essential conditions for human life. A very solid scientific consensus indicates that we are presently witnessing a disturbing warming of the climatic system. In recent decades this warming has been accompanied by a constant rise in the sea level and, it would appear, by an increase of extreme weather events, even if a scientifically determinable cause cannot be assigned to each particular phenomenon. Humanity is called to recognize the need for changes of lifestyle, production and consumption, in order to combat this warming or at least the human causes which produce or aggravate it.

Some Thoughts from Pope Francis

It is true that there are other factors (such as volcanic activity, variations in the earth's orbit and axis, the solar cycle), yet a number of scientific studies indicate that most global warming in recent decades is due to the great concentration of greenhouse gases (carbon dioxide, methane, nitrogen oxides and others) released mainly as a result of human activity. Concentrated in the atmosphere, these gases do not allow the warmth of the sun's rays reflected by the earth to be dispersed in space. The problem is aggravated by a model of development based on the intensive use of fossil fuels, which is at the heart of the worldwide energy system. Another determining factor has been an increase in changed uses of the soil, principally deforestation for agricultural purposes.

24. Warming has effects on the carbon cycle. It creates a vicious circle which aggravates the situation even more, affecting the availability of essential resources like drinking water, energy and agricultural production in warmer regions, and leading to the extinction of part of the planet's biodiversity. The melting in the polar ice caps and in high altitude plains can lead to the dangerous release of methane gas, while the decomposition of frozen organic material can further increase the emission of carbon dioxide. Things are made worse by the loss of tropical forests which would otherwise help to mitigate climate change. Carbon dioxide pollution increases the acidification of the oceans and compromises the marine food chain. If present trends continue, this century may well witness extraordinary climate change and an unprecedented destruction of ecosystems, with serious consequences for all of us. A rise in the sea level, for example, can create extremely serious situations, if we consider that a quarter of the world's population lives on the coast or nearby, and that the majority of our megacities are situated in coastal areas.

25. Climate change is a global problem with grave implications: environmental, social, economic, political and for the distribution of goods. It represents one of the principal challenges facing humanity in our day.

Its worst impact will probably be felt by developing countries in coming decades. Many of the poor live in areas particularly affected by phenomena related to warming, and their means of subsistence are largely dependent on natural reserves and ecosystemic services such as agriculture, fishing and forestry. They have no other financial activities or resources which can enable them to adapt to climate change or to face natural disasters, and their access to social services and protection is very limited. For example, changes in climate, to which animals and plants cannot adapt, lead them to migrate; this in turn affects the livelihood of the poor, who are then forced to leave their homes, with great uncertainty for their future and that of their children. There has been a tragic rise in the number of migrants seeking to flee from the growing poverty caused by environmental degradation. They are not recognized by international conventions as refugees; they bear the loss of the lives they have left behind, without enjoying any legal protection whatsoever. Sadly, there is widespread indifference to such suffering, which is even now taking place throughout our world. Our lack of response to these tragedies involving our brothers and sisters points to the loss of that sense of responsibility for our fellow men and women upon which all civil society is founded.

26. Many of those who possess more resources and economic or political power seem mostly to be concerned with masking the problems or concealing their symptoms, simply making efforts to reduce some of the negative impacts of climate change. However, many of these symptoms indicate that such effects will continue to worsen if we continue with current models of production and consumption. There is an urgent need to develop policies so that, in the next few years, the emission of carbon dioxide and other highly polluting gases can be drastically reduced, for example, substituting for fossil fuels and developing sources of renewable energy.

Worldwide there is minimal access to clean and renewable energy. There is still a need to develop adequate storage technologies. Some countries have made considerable progress, although it is far from constituting a significant proportion. Investments have also been made in means of production and transportation which consume less energy and require fewer raw materials, as well as in methods of construction and renovating buildings which improve their energy efficiency. But these good practices are still far from widespread.

II. The Issue of Water

27. Other indicators of the present situation have to do with the depletion of natural resources. We all know that it is not possible to sustain the present level of consumption in developed countries and wealthier sectors of society, where the habit of wasting and discarding has reached unprecedented levels. The exploitation of the planet has already exceeded acceptable limits and we still have not solved the problem of poverty.

28. Fresh drinking water is an issue of primary importance, since it is indispensable for human life and for supporting terrestrial and aquatic ecosystems. Sources of fresh water are necessary for health care, agriculture and industry. Water supplies used to be relatively constant, but now in many places demand exceeds the sustainable supply, with dramatic consequences in the short and long term. Large cities dependent on significant supplies of water have experienced periods of shortage, and at critical moments these have not always been administered with sufficient oversight and impartiality. Water poverty especially affects Africa where large sectors of the population have no access to safe drinking water or experience droughts which impede agricultural production. Some countries have areas rich in water while others endure drastic scarcity.

29. One particularly serious problem is the quality of water available to the poor. Every day, unsafe water results in many deaths and the spread of water-related diseases, including those caused by microorganisms and chemical substances. Dysentery and cholera, linked to inadequate hygiene and water supplies, are a significant cause of suffering and of infant mortality. Underground water sources in many places are threatened by the pollution produced in certain mining, farming and industrial activities, especially in countries lacking adequate regulation or controls. It is not only a question of industrial waste. Detergents and chemical products, commonly used in many places of the world, continue to pour into our rivers, lakes and seas.

30. Even as the quality of available water is constantly diminishing, in some places there is a growing tendency, despite its scarcity, to privatize this resource, turning it into a commodity subject to the laws of the market. Yet access to safe drinkable water is a basic and universal human right, since it is essential to human survival and, as such, is a condition for the exercise of other human rights. Our world has a grave social debt towards the poor who lack access to drinking water, because they are denied the right to a life consistent with their inalienable dignity. This debt can be paid partly by an increase in funding to provide clean water and sanitary services among the poor. But water continues to be wasted, not only in the developed world but also in developing countries which possess it in abundance. This shows that the problem of water is partly an educational and cultural issue, since there is little awareness of the seriousness of such behavior within a context of great inequality.

31. Greater scarcity of water will lead to an increase in the cost of food and the various products which depend on its use. Some studies warn that an acute water shortage may occur within a few decades unless urgent action is taken. The environmental repercussions could affect billions of people; it is also conceivable that the control of water by large multinational

businesses may become a major source of conflict in this century.

III. Loss of Biodiversity

32. The earth's resources are also being plundered because of short-sighted approaches to the economy, commerce and production. The loss of forests and woodlands entails the loss of species which may constitute extremely important resources in the future, not only for food but also for curing disease and other uses. Different species contain genes which could be key resources in years ahead for meeting human needs and regulating environmental problems.

33. It is not enough, however, to think of different species merely as potential "resources" to be exploited, while overlooking the fact that they have value in themselves. Each year sees the disappearance of thousands of plant and animal species which we will never know, which our children will never see, because they have been lost for ever. The great majority become extinct for reasons related to human activity. Because of us, thousands of species will no longer give glory to God by their very existence, nor convey their message to us. We have no such right.

34. It may well disturb us to learn of the extinction of mammals or birds, since they are more visible. But the good functioning of ecosystems also requires fungi, algae, worms, insects, reptiles and an innumerable variety of microorganisms. Some less numerous species, although generally unseen, nonetheless play a critical role in maintaining the equilibrium of a particular place. Human beings must intervene when a geosystem reaches a critical state. But nowadays, such intervention in nature has become more and more frequent. As a consequence, serious problems arise, leading to further interventions; human activity becomes ubiquitous, with all the risks which this entails. Often a vicious circle results, as human intervention

to resolve a problem further aggravates the situation. For example, many birds and insects which disappear due to synthetic agrotoxins are helpful for agriculture: their disappearance will have to be compensated for by yet other techniques which may well prove harmful. We must be grateful for the praiseworthy efforts being made by scientists and engineers dedicated to finding solutions to man-made problems. But a sober look at our world shows that the degree of human intervention, often in the service of business interests and consumerism, is actually making our earth less rich and beautiful, ever more limited and grey, even as technological advances and consumer goods continue to abound limitlessly. We seem to think that we can substitute an irreplaceable and irretrievable beauty with something which we have created ourselves.

35. In assessing the environmental impact of any project, concern is usually shown for its effects on soil, water and air, yet few careful studies are made of its impact on biodiversity, as if the loss of species or animals and plant groups were of little importance. Highways, new plantations, the fencing-off of certain areas, the damming of water sources, and similar developments, crowd out natural habitats and, at times, break them up in such a way that animal populations can no longer migrate or roam freely. As a result, some species face extinction. Alternatives exist which at least lessen the impact of these projects, like the creation of biological corridors, but few countries demonstrate such concern and foresight. Frequently, when certain species are exploited commercially, little attention is paid to studying their reproductive patterns in order to prevent their depletion and the consequent imbalance of the ecosystem.

36. Caring for ecosystems demands far-sightedness, since no one looking for quick and easy profit is truly interested in their preservation. But the cost of the damage caused by such selfish lack of concern is much greater than the economic benefits to be obtained. Where certain species are destroyed or seriously harmed, the values involved are incalculable. We

can be silent witnesses to terrible injustices if we think that we can obtain significant benefits by making the rest of humanity, present and future, pay the extremely high costs of environmental deterioration.

37. Some countries have made significant progress in establishing sanctuaries on land and in the oceans where any human intervention is prohibited which might modify their features or alter their original structures. In the protection of biodiversity, specialists insist on the need for particular attention to be shown to areas richer both in the number of species and in endemic, rare or less protected species. Certain places need greater protection because of their immense importance for the global ecosystem, or because they represent important water reserves and thus safeguard other forms of life.

38. Let us mention, for example, those richly biodiverse lungs of our planet which are the Amazon and the Congo basins, or the great aquifers and glaciers. We know how important these are for the entire earth and for the future of humanity. The ecosystems of tropical forests possess an enormously complex biodiversity which is almost impossible to appreciate fully, yet when these forests are burned down or levelled for purposes of cultivation, within the space of a few years countless species are lost and the areas frequently become arid wastelands. A delicate balance has to be maintained when speaking about these places, for we cannot overlook the huge global economic interests which, under the guise of protecting them, can undermine the sovereignty of individual nations. In fact, there are "proposals to internationalize the Amazon, which only serve the economic interests of transnational corporations."[3] We cannot fail to praise the commitment of international agencies and civil society organizations which draw public attention to these issues and offer critical cooperation,

---

3   FIFTH GENERAL CONFERENCE OF THE LATIN AMERICAN AND CA-RIBBEAN BISHOPS,
Aparecida Document (29 June 2007), 86.

employing legitimate means of pressure, to ensure that each government carries out its proper and inalienable responsibility to preserve its country's environment and natural resources, without capitulating to spurious local or international interests.

39. The replacement of virgin forest with plantations of trees, usually monocultures, is rarely adequately analyzed. Yet this can seriously compromise a biodiversity which the new species being introduced does not accommodate. Similarly, wetlands converted into cultivated land lose the enormous biodiversity which they formerly hosted. In some coastal areas the disappearance of ecosystems sustained by mangrove swamps is a source of serious concern.

40. Oceans not only contain the bulk of our planet's water supply, but also most of the immense variety of living creatures, many of them still unknown to us and threatened for various reasons. What is more, marine life in rivers, lakes, seas and oceans, which feeds a great part of the world's population, is affected by uncontrolled fishing, leading to a drastic depletion of certain species. Selective forms of fishing which discard much of what they collect continue unabated. Particularly threatened are marine organisms which we tend to overlook, like some forms of plankton; they represent a significant element in the ocean food chain, and species used for our food ultimately depend on them.

41. In tropical and subtropical seas, we find coral reefs comparable to the great forests on dry land, for they shelter approximately a million species, including fish, crabs, molluscs, sponges and algae. Many of the world's coral reefs are already barren or in a state of constant decline. "Who turned the wonderworld of the seas into underwater cemeteries bereft of colour and life?"[4] This phenomenon is due largely to pollution which

---

4   CATHOLIC BISHOPS' CONFERENCE OF THE PHILIPPINES, Pastoral Letter What is Happening to our Beautiful Land? (29 January 1988).

reaches the sea as the result of deforestation, agricultural monocultures, industrial waste and destructive fishing methods, especially those using cyanide and dynamite. It is aggravated by the rise in temperature of the oceans. All of this helps us to see that every intervention in nature can have consequences which are not immediately evident, and that certain ways of exploiting resources prove costly in terms of degradation which ultimately reaches the ocean bed itself.

42. Greater investment needs to be made in research aimed at understanding more fully the functioning of ecosystems and adequately analyzing the different variables associated with any significant modification of the environment. Because all creatures are connected, each must be cherished with love and respect, for all of us as living creatures are dependent on one another. Each area is responsible for the care of this family. This will require undertaking a careful inventory of the species which it hosts, with a view to developing programmes and strategies of protection with particular care for safeguarding species heading towards extinction.

IV. Decline in the Equality of Human Life and the Breakdown of Society

43. Human beings too are creatures of this world, enjoying a right to life and happiness, and endowed with unique dignity. So we cannot fail to consider the effects on people's lives of environmental deterioration, current models of development and the throwaway culture.

44. Nowadays, for example, we are conscious of the disproportionate and unruly growth of many cities, which have become unhealthy to live in, not only because of pollution caused by toxic emissions but also as a result of urban chaos, poor transportation, and visual pollution and noise. Many cities are huge, inefficient structures, excessively wasteful of energy and

water. Neighbourhoods, even those recently built, are congested, chaotic and lacking in sufficient green space. We were not meant to be inundated by cement, asphalt, glass and metal, and deprived of physical contact with nature.

45. In some places, rural and urban alike, the privatization of certain spaces has restricted people's access to places of particular beauty. In others, "ecological" neighbourhoods have been created which are closed to outsiders in order to ensure an artificial tranquillity. Frequently, we find beautiful and carefully manicured green spaces in so-called "safer" areas of cities, but not in the more hidden areas where the disposable of society live.

46. The social dimensions of global change include the effects of technological innovations on employment, social exclusion, an inequitable distribution and consumption of energy and other services, social breakdown, increased violence and a rise in new forms of social aggression, drug trafficking, growing drug use by young people, and the loss of identity. These are signs that the growth of the past two centuries has not always led to an integral development and an improvement in the quality of life. Some of these signs are also symptomatic of real social decline, the silent rupture of the bonds of integration and social cohesion.

47. Furthermore, when media and the digital world become omnipresent, their influence can stop people from learning how to live wisely, to think deeply and to love generously. In this context, the great sages of the past run the risk of going unheard amid the noise and distractions of an information overload. Efforts need to be made to help these media become sources of new cultural progress for humanity and not a threat to our deepest riches. True wisdom, as the fruit of self-examination, dialogue and generous encounter between persons, is not acquired by a mere accumulation of data which eventually leads to overload and confusion, a sort of mental

pollution. Real relationships with others, with all the challenges they entail, now tend to be replaced by a type of internet communication which enables us to choose or eliminate relationships at whim, thus giving rise to a new type of contrived emotion which has more to do with devices and displays than with other people and with nature. Today's media do enable us to communicate and to share our knowledge and affections. Yet at times they also shield us from direct contact with the pain, the fears and the joys of others and the complexity of their personal experiences. For this reason, we should be concerned that, alongside the exciting possibilities offered by these media, a deep and melancholic dissatisfaction with interpersonal relations, or a harmful sense of isolation, can also arise.

V. Global Inequality

48. The human environment and the natural environment deteriorate together; we cannot adequately combat environmental degradation unless we attend to causes related to human and social degradation. In fact, the deterioration of the environment and of society affects the most vulnerable people on the planet: "Both everyday experience and scientific research show that the gravest effects of all attacks on the environment are suffered by the poorest."[5] For example, the depletion of fishing reserves especially hurts small fishing communities without the means to replace those resources; water pollution particularly affects the poor who cannot buy bottled water; and rises in the sea level mainly affect impoverished coastal populations who have nowhere else to go. The impact of present imbalances is also seen in the premature death of many of the poor, in conflicts sparked by the shortage of resources, and in any number of other

---

5 BOLIVIAN BISHOPS' CONFERENCE, Pastoral Letter on the Environment and Human Development in Bolivia El universo, don de Dios para la vida (23 March 2012), 17.

problems which are insufficiently represented on global agendas.

49. It needs to be said that, generally speaking, there is little in the way of clear awareness of problems which especially affect the excluded. Yet they are the majority of the planet's population, billions of people. These days, they are mentioned in international political and economic discussions, but one often has the impression that their problems are brought up as an afterthought, a question which gets added almost out of duty or in a tangential way, if not treated merely as collateral damage. Indeed, when all is said and done, they frequently remain at the bottom of the pile. This is due partly to the fact that many professionals, opinion makers, communications media and centers of power, being located in affluent urban areas, are far removed from the poor, with little direct contact with their problems. They live and reason from the comfortable position of a high level of development and a quality of life well beyond the reach of the majority of the world's population. This lack of physical contact and encounter, encouraged at times by the disintegration of our cities, can lead to a numbing of conscience and to tendentious analyses which neglect parts of reality. At times this attitude exists side by side with a "green" rhetoric. Today, however, we have to realize that a true ecological approach always becomes a social approach; it must integrate questions of justice in debates on the environment, so as to hear both the cry of the earth and the cry of the poor.

50. Instead of resolving the problems of the poor and thinking of how the world can be different, some can only propose a reduction in the birth rate. At times, developing countries face forms of international pressure which make economic assistance contingent on certain policies of "reproductive health." Yet "while it is true that an unequal distribution of the population and of available resources creates obstacles to development and a sustainable use of the environment, it must nonetheless be recognized that demographic growth is fully compatible with an integral and shared

development."[6] To blame population growth instead of extreme and selective consumerism on the part of some, is one way of refusing to face the issues. It is an attempt to legitimize the present model of distribution, where a minority believes that it has the right to consume in a way which can never be universalized, since the planet could not even contain the waste products of such consumption. Besides, we know that approximately a third of all food produced is discarded, and "whenever food is thrown out it is as if it were stolen from the table of the poor."[7] Still, attention needs to be paid to imbalances in population density, on both national and global levels, since a rise in consumption would lead to complex regional situations, as a result of the interplay between problems linked to environmental pollution, transport, waste treatment, loss of resources and quality of life.

51. Inequity affects not only individuals but entire countries; it compels us to consider an ethics of international relations. A true "ecological debt" exists, particularly between the global north and south, connected to commercial imbalances with effects on the environment, and the disproportionate use of natural resources by certain countries over long periods of time. The export of raw materials to satisfy markets in the industrialized north has caused harm locally, as for example in mercury pollution in gold mining or sulphur dioxide pollution in copper mining. There is a pressing need to calculate the use of environmental space throughout the world for depositing gas residues which have been accumulating for two centuries and have created a situation which currently affects all the countries of the world. The warming caused by huge consumption on the part of some rich countries has repercussions on the poorest areas of the world, especially Africa, where a rise in temperature, together with drought, has proved devastating

---

6   PONTIFICAL COUNCIL FOR JUSTICE AND PEACE, Compendium of the Social Doctrine of the Church, 483.

7   Catechesis (5 June 2013): Insegnamenti 1/1 (2013), 280.

for farming. There is also the damage caused by the export of solid waste and toxic liquids to developing countries, and by the pollution produced by companies which operate in less developed countries in ways they could never do at home, in the countries in which they raise their capital: "We note that often the businesses which operate this way are multinationals. They do here what they would never do in developed countries or the so-called first world. Generally, after ceasing their activity and withdrawing, they leave behind great human and environmental liabilities such as unemployment, abandoned towns, the depletion of natural reserves, deforestation, the impoverishment of agriculture and local stock breeding, open pits, riven hills, polluted rivers and a handful of social works which are no longer sustainable."[8]

52. The foreign debt of poor countries has become a way of controlling them, yet this is not the case where ecological debt is concerned. In different ways, developing countries, where the most important reserves of the biosphere are found, continue to fuel the development of richer countries at the cost of their own present and future. The land of the southern poor is rich and mostly unpolluted, yet access to ownership of goods and resources for meeting vital needs is inhibited by a system of commercial relations and ownership which is structurally perverse. The developed countries ought to help pay this debt by significantly limiting their consumption of non-renewable energy and by assisting poorer countries to support policies and programmes of sustainable development. The poorest areas and countries are less capable of adopting new models for reducing environmental impact because they lack the wherewithal to develop the necessary processes and to cover their costs. We must continue to be aware that, regarding climate change, there are differentiated responsibilities. As the United States

---

8 BISHOPS OF THE PATAGONIA-COMAHUE REGION (ARGENTINA), Christmas Message
(December 2009), 2.

bishops have said, greater attention must be given to "the needs of the poor, the weak and the vulnerable, in a debate often dominated by more powerful interests."[9] We need to strengthen the conviction that we are one single human family. There are no frontiers or barriers, political or social, behind which we can hide, still less is there room for the globalization of indifference.

VI. Weak Responses

53. These situations have caused sister earth, along with all the abandoned of our world, to cry out, pleading that we take another course. Never have we so hurt and mistreated our common home as we have in the last two hundred years. Yet we are called to be instruments of God our Father, so that our planet might be what he desired when he created it and correspond with his plan for peace, beauty and fullness. The problem is that we still lack the culture needed to confront this crisis. We lack leadership capable of striking out on new paths and meeting the needs of the present with concern for all and without prejudice towards coming generations. The establishment of a legal framework which can set clear boundaries and ensure the protection of ecosystems has become indispensable; otherwise, the new power structures based on the techno-economic paradigm may overwhelm not only our politics but also freedom and justice.

54. It is remarkable how weak international political responses have been. The failure of global summits on the environment make it plain that our politics are subject to technology and finance. There are too many special interests, and economic interests easily end up trumping the common good and manipulating information so that their own plans will not be

---

9 UNITED STATES CONFERENCE OF CATHOLIC BISHOPS, Global Climate Change: A Plea for Dialogue, Prudence and the Common Good (15 June 2001).

affected. The Aparecida Document urges that "the interests of economic groups which irrationally demolish sources of life should not prevail in dealing with natural resources."[10] The alliance between the economy and technology ends up sidelining anything unrelated to its immediate interests. Consequently the most one can expect is superficial rhetoric, sporadic acts of philanthropy and perfunctory expressions of concern for the environment, whereas any genuine attempt by groups within society to introduce change is viewed as a nuisance based on romantic illusions or an obstacle to be circumvented.

55. Some countries are gradually making significant progress, developing more effective controls and working to combat corruption. People may well have a growing ecological sensitivity but it has not succeeded in changing their harmful habits of consumption which, rather than decreasing, appear to be growing all the more. A simple example is the increasing use and power of air- conditioning. The markets, which immediately benefit from sales, stimulate ever greater demand. An outsider looking at our world would be amazed at such behavior, which at times appears self- destructive.

56. In the meantime, economic powers continue to justify the current global system where priority tends to be given to speculation and the pursuit of financial gain, which fail to take the context into account, let alone the effects on human dignity and the natural environment. Here we see how environmental deterioration and human and ethical degradation are closely linked. Many people will deny doing anything wrong because distractions constantly dull our consciousness of just how limited and finite our world really is. As a result, "whatever is fragile, like the environment, is defenceless before the interests of a deified market, which become the only rule."[11]

---

10 FIFTH GENERAL CONFERENCE OF THE LATIN AMERICAN AND CA-RIBBEAN BISHOPS, Aparecida Document (29 June 2007), 471.

11 Apostolic Exhortation Evangelii Gaudium (24 November 2013), 56: AAS

57. It is foreseeable that, once certain resources have been depleted, the scene will be set for new wars, albeit under the guise of noble claims. War always does grave harm to the environment and to the cultural riches of peoples, risks which are magnified when one considers nuclear arms and biological weapons. "Despite the international agreements which prohibit chemical, bacteriological and biological warfare, the fact is that laboratory research continues to develop new offensive weapons capable of altering the balance of nature."[12] Politics must pay greater attention to foreseeing new conflicts and addressing the causes which can lead to them. But powerful financial interests prove most resistant to this effort, and political planning tends to lack breadth of vision. What would induce anyone, at this stage, to hold on to power only to be remembered for their inability to take action when it was urgent and necessary to do so?

58. In some countries, there are positive examples of environmental improvement: rivers, polluted for decades, have been cleaned up; native woodlands have been restored; landscapes have been beautified thanks to environmental renewal projects; beautiful buildings have been erected; advances have been made in the production of non-polluting energy and in the improvement of public transportation. These achievements do not solve global problems, but they do show that men and women are still capable of intervening positively. For all our limitations, gestures of generosity, solidarity and care cannot but well up within us, since we were made for love.

59. At the same time we can note the rise of a false or superficial ecology which bolsters complacency and a cheerful recklessness. As often occurs in periods of deep crisis which require bold decisions, we are tempted to think that what is happening is not entirely clear. Superficially, apart

---

105 (2013), 1043.

12 JOHN PAUL II, Message for the 1990 World Day of Peace, 12: AAS 82 (1990), 154.

from a few obvious signs of pollution and deterioration, things do not look that serious, and the planet could continue as it is for some time. Such evasiveness serves as a licence to carrying on with our present lifestyles and models of production and consumption. This is the way human beings contrive to feed their self-destructive vices: trying not to see them, trying not to acknowledge them, delaying the important decisions and pretending that nothing will happen.

VII. A Variety of Opinions

60. Finally, we need to acknowledge that different approaches and lines of thought have emerged regarding this situation and its possible solutions. At one extreme, we find those who doggedly uphold the myth of progress and tell us that ecological problems will solve themselves simply with the application of new technology and without any need for ethical considerations or deep change. At the other extreme are those who view men and women and all their interventions as no more than a threat, jeopardizing the global ecosystem, and consequently the presence of human beings on the planet should be reduced and all forms of intervention prohibited. Viable future scenarios will have to be generated between these extremes, since there is no one path to a solution. This makes a variety of proposals possible, all capable of entering into dialogue with a view to developing comprehensive solutions.

61. On many concrete questions, the Church has no reason to offer a definitive opinion; she knows that honest debate must be encouraged among experts, while respecting divergent views. But we need only take a frank look at the facts to see that our common home is falling into serious disrepair. Hope would have us recognize that there is always a way out, that we can always redirect our steps, that we can always do something to solve our problems. Still, we can see signs that things are now reaching a

breaking point, due to the rapid pace of change and degradation; these are evident in large-scale natural disasters as well as social and even financial crises, for the world's problems cannot be analyzed or explained in isolation. There are regions now at high risk and, aside from all doomsday predictions, the present world system is certainly unsustainable from a number of points of view, for we have stopped thinking about the goals of human activity. "If we scan the regions of our planet, we immediately see that humanity has disappointed God's expectations."[13]

67. We are not God. The earth was here before us and it has been given to us. This allows us to respond to the charge that Judaeo-Christian thinking, on the basis of the Genesis account which grants man "dominion" over the earth (cf. Gen 1:28), has encouraged the unbridled exploitation of nature by painting him as domineering and destructive by nature. This is not a correct interpretation of the Bible as understood by the Church. Although it is true that we Christians have at times incorrectly interpreted the Scriptures, nowadays we must forcefully reject the notion that our being created in God's image and given dominion over the earth justifies absolute domination over other creatures. The biblical texts are to be read in their context, with an appropriate hermeneutic, recognizing that they tell us to "till and keep" the garden of the world (cf. Gen 2:15). "Tilling" refers to cultivating, ploughing or working, while "keeping" means caring, protecting, overseeing and preserving. This implies a relationship of mutual responsibility between human beings and nature. Each community can take from the bounty of the earth whatever it needs for subsistence, but it also has the duty to protect the earth and to ensure its fruitfulness for coming generations. "The earth is the Lord's" (Ps 24:1); to him belongs "the earth with all that is within it" (Dt 10:14). Thus God rejects every claim to absolute ownership: "The land shall not be sold in perpetuity,

---

13 Catechesis (17 January 2001), 3: Insegnamenti 24/1 (2001), 178.

for the land is mine; for you are strangers and sojourners with me" (Lev 25:23).

68. This responsibility for God's earth means that human beings, endowed with intelligence, must respect the laws of nature and the delicate equilibria existing between the creatures of this world, for "he commanded and they were created; and he established them for ever and ever; he fixed their bounds and he set a law which cannot pass away" (Ps 148:5b-6). The laws found in the Bible dwell on relationships, not only among individuals but also with other living beings. "You shall not see your brother's donkey or his ox fallen down by the way and withhold your help... If you chance to come upon a bird's nest in any tree or on the ground, with young ones or eggs and the mother sitting upon the young or upon the eggs; you shall not take the mother with the young" (Dt 22:4, 6). Along these same lines, rest on the seventh day is meant not only for human beings, but also so "that your ox and your donkey may have rest" (Ex 23:12). Clearly, the Bible has no place for a tyrannical anthropocentrism unconcerned for other creatures.

69. Together with our obligation to use the earth's goods responsibly, we are called to recognize that other living beings have a value of their own in God's eyes: "by their mere existence they bless him and give him glory,"[14] and indeed, "the Lord rejoices in all his works" (Ps 104:31). By virtue of our unique dignity and our gift of intelligence, we are called to respect creation and its inherent laws, for "the Lord by wisdom founded the earth" (Prov 3:19). In our time, the Church does not simply state that other creatures are completely subordinated to the good of human beings, as if they have no worth in themselves and can be treated as we wish. The German bishops have taught that, where other creatures are concerned, "we can speak of the priority of being over that of being useful."[15] The Catechism clearly

---

14 Catechism of the Catholic Church, 2416.

15 GERMAN BISHOPS' CONFERENCE, Zukunft der Schöpfung – Zukunft der

and forcefully criticizes a distorted anthropocentrism: "Each creature possesses its own particular goodness and perfection... Each of the various creatures, willed in its own being, reflects in its own way a ray of God's infinite wisdom and goodness. Man must therefore respect the particular goodness of every creature, to avoid any disordered use of things."[16]

Menschheit. Einklärung der Deutschen Bischofskonferenz zu Fragen der Umwelt und der Energieversorgung, (1980), II, 2.

16 Catechism of the Catholic Church, 339.

78. [Judaeo-Christian thought] demythologized nature. While continuing to admire its grandeur and immensity, it no longer saw nature as divine. In doing so, it emphasizes all the more our human responsibility for nature. This rediscovery of nature can never be at the cost of the freedom and responsibility of human beings who, as part of the world, have the duty to cultivate their abilities in order to protect it and develop its potential. If we acknowledge the value and the fragility of nature and, at the same time, our God-given abilities, we can finally leave behind the modern myth of unlimited material progress. A fragile world, entrusted by God to human care, challenges us to devise intelligent ways of directing, developing and limiting our power.

81. Human beings, even if we postulate a process of evolution, also possess a uniqueness which cannot be fully explained by the evolution of other open systems. Each of us has his or her own personal identity and is capable of entering into dialogue with others and with God himself. Our capacity to reason, to develop arguments, to be inventive, to interpret reality and to create art, along with other not yet discovered capacities, are signs of a uniqueness which transcends the spheres of physics and biology. The sheer novelty involved in the emergence of a personal being within a material universe presupposes a direct action of God and a particular call to life and to relationship on the part of a "Thou" who addresses himself to another "thou." The biblical accounts of creation invite us to see each human being as a subject who can never be reduced to the status of an object.

82. Yet it would also be mistaken to view other living beings as mere objects subjected to arbitrary human domination. When nature is viewed solely as a source of profit and gain, this has serious consequences for society. This vision of "might is right" has engendered immense inequality, injustice

and acts of violence against the majority of humanity, since resources end up in the hands of the first comer or the most powerful: the winner takes all. Completely at odds with this model are the ideals of harmony, justice, fraternity and peace as proposed by Jesus. As he said of the powers of his own age: "You know that the rulers of the Gentiles lord it over them, and their great men exercise authority over them. It shall not be so among you; but whoever would be great among you must be your servant" (Mt 20:25-26).

VI. The Common Destination of Good

93. Whether believers or not, we are agreed today that the earth is essentially a shared inheritance, whose fruits are meant to benefit everyone. For believers, this becomes a question of fidelity to the Creator, since God created the world for everyone. Hence every ecological approach needs to incorporate a social perspective which takes into account the fundamental rights of the poor and the underprivileged. The principle of the subordination of private property to the universal destination of goods, and thus the right of everyone to their use, is a golden rule of social conduct and "the first principle of the whole ethical and social order."[17] The Christian tradition has never recognized the right to private property as absolute or inviolable, and has stressed the social purpose of all forms of private property.

94. The rich and the poor have equal dignity, for "the Lord is the maker of them all" (Prov 22:2). "He himself made both small and great" (Wis 6:7), and "he makes his sun rise on the evil and on the good" (Mt 5:45). This has practical consequences, such as those pointed out by the bishops of Paraguay: "Every campesino has a natural right to possess a reasonable

---

17 JOHN PAUL II, Encyclical Letter Laborem Exercens (14 September 1981), 19: AAS 73 (1981), 626.

allotment of land where he can establish his home, work for subsistence of his family and a secure life. This right must be guaranteed so that its exercise is not illusory but real. That means that apart from the ownership of property, rural people must have access to means of technical education, credit, insurance, and markets."[18]

95. The natural environment is a collective good, the patrimony of all humanity and the responsibility of everyone. If we make something our own, it is only to administer it for the good of all. If we do not, we burden our consciences with the weight of having denied the existence of others. That is why the New Zealand bishops asked what the commandment "Thou shall not kill" means when "twenty percent of the world's population consumes resources at a rate that robs the poor nations and future generations of what they need to survive."[19]

THE HUMAN ROOTS OF THE ECOLOGICAL CRISIS

101. It would hardly be helpful to describe symptoms without acknowledging the human origins of the ecological crisis. A certain way of understanding human life and activity has gone awry, to the serious detriment of the world around us. Should we not pause and consider this? At this stage, I propose that we focus on the dominant technocratic paradigm and the place of human beings and of human action in the world.

---

18 PARAGUAYAN BISHOPS' CONFERENCE, Pastoral Letter El campesino paraguayo y la tierra (12 June 1983), 2, 4, d.
19 NEW ZEALAND CATHOLIC BISHOPS CONFERENCE, Statement on Environmental Issues (1 September 2006).

Some Thoughts from Pope Francis

I. Technology: Creativity and Power

102. Humanity has entered a new era in which our technical prowess has brought us to a crossroads. We are the beneficiaries of two centuries of enormous waves of change: steam engines, railways, the telegraph, electricity, automobiles, aeroplanes, chemical industries, modern medicine, information technology and, more recently, the digital revolution, robotics, biotechnologies and nanotechnologies. It is right to rejoice in these advances and to be excited by the immense possibilities which they continue to open up before us, for "science and technology are wonderful products of a God-given human creativity."[20] The modification of nature for useful purposes has distinguished the human family from the beginning; technology itself "expresses the inner tension that impels man gradually to overcome material limitations."[21] Technology has remedied countless evils which used to harm and limit human beings. How can we not feel gratitude and appreciation for this progress, especially in the fields of medicine, engineering and communications? How could we not acknowledge the work of many scientists and engineers who have provided alternatives to make development sustainable?

103. Technoscience, when well directed, can produce important means of improving the quality of human life, from useful domestic appliances to great transportation systems, bridges, buildings and public spaces. It can also produce art and enable men and women immersed in the material world to "leap" into the world of beauty. Who can deny the beauty of an aircraft or a skyscraper? Valuable works of art and music now make use

---

20 JOHN PAUL II, Address to Scientists and Representatives of the United Nations University, Hiroshima (25 February 1981), 3: AAS 73 (1981), 42.
21 BENEDICT XVI, Encyclical Letter Caritas in Veritate (29 June 2009), 69: AAS 101 (2009), 702.

of new technologies. So, in the beauty intended by the one who uses new technical instruments and in the contemplation of such beauty, a quantum leap occurs, resulting in a fulfilment which is uniquely human.

104. Yet it must also be recognized that nuclear energy, biotechnology, information technology, knowledge of our DNA, and many other abilities which we have acquired, have given us tremendous power. More precisely, they have given those with the knowledge, and especially the economic resources to use them, an impressive dominance over the whole of humanity and the entire world. Never has humanity had such power over itself, yet nothing ensures that it will be used wisely, particularly when we consider how it is currently being used. We need but think of the nuclear bombs dropped in the middle of the twentieth century, or the array of technology which Nazism, Communism and other totalitarian regimes have employed to kill millions of people, to say nothing of the increasingly deadly arsenal of weapons available for modern warfare. In whose hands does all this power lie, or will it eventually end up? It is extremely risky for a small part of humanity to have it.

105. There is a tendency to believe that every increase in power means "an increase of 'progress' itself," an advance in "security, usefulness, welfare and vigour; ...an assimilation of new values into the stream of culture,"[22] as if reality, goodness and truth automatically flow from technological and economic power as such. The fact is that "contemporary man has not been trained to use power well,"[23] because our immense technological development has not been accompanied by a development in human responsibility, values and conscience. Each age tends to have only a meagre awareness of its own limitations. It is possible that we do not grasp the gravity of the challenges now before us. "The risk is growing day by

---

22 ROMANO GUARDINI, Das Ende der Neuzeit, 9th ed., Würzburg, 1965, 87 (English: The End of the Modern World, Wilmington, 1998, 82).
23 Ibid.

day that man will not use his power as he should"; in effect, "power is never considered in terms of the responsibility of choice which is inherent in freedom" since its "only norms are taken from alleged necessity, from either utility or security."[24] But human beings are not completely autonomous. Our freedom fades when it is handed over to the blind forces of the unconscious, of immediate needs, of self-interest, and of violence. In this sense, we stand naked and exposed in the face of our ever-increasing power, lacking the wherewithal to control it. We have certain superficial mechanisms, but we cannot claim to have a sound ethics, a culture and spirituality genuinely capable of setting limits and teaching clear-minded self-restraint.

II. The Globalization of the Technocratic Paradigm

106. The basic problem goes even deeper: it is the way that humanity has taken up technology and its development according to an undifferentiated and one-dimensional paradigm. This paradigm exalts the concept of a subject who, using logical and rational procedures, progressively approaches and gains control over an external object. This subject makes every effort to establish the scientific and experimental method, which in itself is already a technique of possession, mastery and transformation. It is as if the subject were to find itself in the presence of something formless, completely open to manipulation. Men and women have constantly intervened in nature, but for a long time this meant being in tune with and respecting the possibilities offered by the things themselves. It was a matter of receiving what nature itself allowed, as if from its own hand. Now, by contrast, we are the ones to lay our hands on things, attempting to extract everything possible from them while frequently ignoring or forgetting the reality in front of us. Human beings and material objects no

---

24   bid., 87-88 (The End of the Modern World, 83).

longer extend a friendly hand to one another; the relationship has become confrontational. This has made it easy to accept the idea of infinite or unlimited growth, which proves so attractive to economists, financiers and experts in technology. It is based on the lie that there is an infinite supply of the earth's goods, and this leads to the planet being squeezed dry beyond every limit. It is the false notion that "an infinite quantity of energy and resources are available, that it is possible to renew them quickly, and that the negative effects of the exploitation of the natural order can be easily absorbed."[25]

107. It can be said that many problems of today's world stem from the tendency, at times unconscious, to make the method and aims of science and technology an epistemological paradigm which shapes the lives of individuals and the workings of society. The effects of imposing this model on reality as a whole, human and social, are seen in the deterioration of the environment, but this is just one sign of a reductionism which affects every aspect of human and social life. We have to accept that technological products are not neutral, for they create a framework which ends up conditioning lifestyles and shaping social possibilities along the lines dictated by the interests of certain powerful groups. Decisions which may seem purely instrumental are in reality decisions about the kind of society we want to build.

108. The idea of promoting a different cultural paradigm and employing technology as a mere instrument is nowadays inconceivable. The technological paradigm has become so dominant that it would be difficult to do without its resources and even more difficult to utilize them without being dominated by their internal logic. It has become countercultural to choose a lifestyle whose goals are even partly independent of technology, of its costs and its power to globalize and make us all the same. Technology

---

25 PONTIFICAL COUNCIL FOR JUSTICE AND PEACE, Compendium of the Social Doctrine of the Church, 462.

tends to absorb everything into its ironclad logic, and those who are surrounded with technology "know full well that it moves forward in the final analysis neither for profit nor for the well-being of the human race," that "in the most radical sense of the term power is its motive – a lordship over all."[26] As a result, "man seizes hold of the naked elements of both nature and human nature."[27] Our capacity to make decisions, a more genuine freedom and the space for each one's alternative creativity are diminished.

109. The technocratic paradigm also tends to dominate economic and political life. The economy accepts every advance in technology with a view to profit, without concern for its potentially negative impact on human beings. Finance overwhelms the real economy. The lessons of the global financial crisis have not been assimilated, and we are learning all too slowly the lessons of environmental deterioration. Some circles maintain that current economics and technology will solve all environmental problems, and argue, in popular and non-technical terms, that the problems of global hunger and poverty will be resolved simply by market growth. They are less concerned with certain economic theories which today scarcely anybody dares defend, than with their actual operation in the functioning of the economy. They may not affirm such theories with words, but nonetheless support them with their deeds by showing no interest in more balanced levels of production, a better distribution of wealth, concern for the environment and the rights of future generations. Their behavior shows that for them maximizing profits is enough. Yet by itself the market cannot guarantee integral human development and social inclusion. At the same time, we have "a sort of 'superdevelopment' of a wasteful and consumerist kind which forms an unacceptable contrast with the ongoing situations

---

26   ROMANO GUARDINI, Das Ende der Neuzeit, 63-64 (The End of the Modern World, 56).

27   Ibid., 64 (The End of the Modern World, 56).

of dehumanizing deprivation,"[28] while we are all too slow in developing economic institutions and social initiatives which can give the poor regular access to basic resources. We fail to see the deepest roots of our present failures, which have to do with the direction, goals, meaning and social implications of technological and economic growth.

110. The specialization which belongs to technology makes it difficult to see the larger picture. The fragmentation of knowledge proves helpful for concrete applications, and yet it often leads to a loss of appreciation for the whole, for the relationships between things, and for the broader horizon, which then becomes irrelevant. This very fact makes it hard to find adequate ways of solving the more complex problems of today's world, particularly those regarding the environment and the poor; these problems cannot be dealt with from a single perspective or from a single set of interests. A science which would offer solutions to the great issues would necessarily have to take into account the data generated by other fields of knowledge, including philosophy and social ethics; but this is a difficult habit to acquire today. Nor are there genuine ethical horizons to which one can appeal. Life gradually becomes a surrender to situations conditioned by technology, itself viewed as the principal key to the meaning of existence. In the concrete situation confronting us, there are a number of symptoms which point to what is wrong, such as environmental degradation, anxiety, a loss of the purpose of life and of community living. Once more we see that "realities are more important than ideas."[29]

111. Ecological culture cannot be reduced to a series of urgent and partial responses to the immediate problems of pollution, environmental decay and the depletion of natural resources. There needs to be a distinctive way of looking at things, a way of thinking, policies, an educational programme,

---

28 Ibid., 22: p. 657.
29 Apostolic Exhortation *Evangelii Gaudium* (24 November 2013), 231: AAS 105 (2013), 1114.

a lifestyle and a spirituality which together generate resistance to the assault of the technocratic paradigm. Otherwise, even the best ecological initiatives can find themselves caught up in the same globalized logic. To seek only a technical remedy to each environmental problem which comes up is to separate what is in reality interconnected and to mask the true and deepest problems of the global system.

112. Yet we can once more broaden our vision. We have the freedom needed to limit and direct technology; we can put it at the service of another type of progress, one which is healthier, more human, more social, more integral. Liberation from the dominant technocratic paradigm does in fact happen sometimes, for example, when cooperatives of small producers adopt less polluting means of production, and opt for a non-consumerist model of life, recreation and community. Or when technology is directed primarily to resolving people's concrete problems, truly helping them live with more dignity and less suffering. Or indeed when the desire to create and contemplate beauty manages to overcome reductionism through a kind of salvation which occurs in beauty and in those who behold it. An authentic humanity, calling for a new synthesis, seems to dwell in the midst of our technological culture, almost unnoticed, like a mist seeping gently beneath a closed door. Will the promise last, in spite of everything, with all that is authentic rising up in stubborn resistance?

113. There is also the fact that people no longer seem to believe in a happy future; they no longer have blind trust in a better tomorrow based on the present state of the world and our technical abilities. There is a growing awareness that scientific and technological progress cannot be equated with the progress of humanity and history, a growing sense that the way to a better future lies elsewhere. This is not to reject the possibilities which technology continues to offer us. But humanity has changed profoundly, and the accumulation of constant novelties exalts a superficiality which pulls us in one direction. It becomes difficult to pause and recover depth

in life. If architecture reflects the spirit of an age, our megastructures and drab apartment blocks express the spirit of globalized technology, where a constant flood of new products coexists with a tedious monotony. Let us refuse to resign ourselves to this, and continue to wonder about the purpose and meaning of everything. Otherwise we would simply legitimate the present situation and need new forms of escapism to help us endure the emptiness.

114. All of this shows the urgent need for us to move forward in a bold cultural revolution. Science and technology are not neutral; from the beginning to the end of a process, various intentions and possibilities are in play and can take on distinct shapes. Nobody is suggesting a return to the Stone Age, but we do need to slow down and look at reality in a different way, to appropriate the positive and sustainable progress which has been made, but also to recover the values and the great goals swept away by our unrestrained delusions of grandeur.

III. The Crisis and Effects of Modern Anthropocentrism

115. Modern anthropocentrism has paradoxically ended up prizing technical thought over reality, since "the technological mind sees nature as an insensate order, as a cold body of facts, as a mere 'given', as an object of utility, as raw material to be hammered into useful shape; it views the cosmos similarly as a mere 'space' into which objects can be thrown with complete indifference."[30] The intrinsic dignity of the world is thus compromised. When human beings fail to find their true place in this world, they misunderstand themselves and end up acting against themselves: "Not only has God given the earth to man, who must use it with respect for the original good purpose for which it was given, but, man

---

30 ROMANO GUARDINI, Das Ende der Neuzeit, 63 (The End of the Modern World, 55).

too is God's gift to man. He must therefore respect the natural and moral structure with which he has been endowed."[31]

116. Modernity has been marked by an excessive anthropocentrism which today, under another guise, continues to stand in the way of shared understanding and of any effort to strengthen social bonds. The time has come to pay renewed attention to reality and the limits it imposes; this in turn is the condition for a more sound and fruitful development of individuals and society. An inadequate presentation of Christian anthropology gave rise to a wrong understanding of the relationship between human beings and the world. Often, what was handed on was a Promethean vision of mastery over the world, which gave the impression that the protection of nature was something that only the faint-hearted cared about. Instead, our "dominion" over the universe should be understood more properly in the sense of responsible stewardship.

117. Neglecting to monitor the harm done to nature and the environmental impact of our decisions is only the most striking sign of a disregard for the message contained in the structures of nature itself. When we fail to acknowledge as part of reality the worth of a poor person, a human embryo, a person with disabilities – to offer just a few examples – it becomes difficult to hear the cry of nature itself; everything is connected. Once the human being declares independence from reality and behaves with absolute dominion, the very foundations of our life begin to crumble, for "instead of carrying out his role as a cooperator with God in the work of creation, man sets himself up in place of God and thus ends up provoking a rebellion on the part of nature."[32]

---

31   JOHN PAUL II, Encyclical Letter Centesimus Annus (1 May 1991), 38: AAS 83 (1991), 841.

32   JOHN PAUL II, Encyclical Letter Centesimus Annus (1 May 1991), 37: AAS 83 (1991), 840.

118. This situation has led to a constant schizophrenia, wherein a technocracy which sees no intrinsic value in lesser beings coexists with the other extreme, which sees no special value in human beings. But one cannot prescind from humanity. There can be no renewal of our relationship with nature without a renewal of humanity itself. There can be no ecology without an adequate anthropology. When the human person is considered as simply one being among others, the product of chance or physical determinism, then "our overall sense of responsibility wanes."[33] A misguided anthropocentrism need not necessarily yield to "biocentrism," for that would entail adding yet another imbalance, failing to solve present problems and adding new ones. Human beings cannot be expected to feel responsibility for the world unless, at the same time, their unique capacities of knowledge, will, freedom and responsibility are recognized and valued.

119. Nor must the critique of a misguided anthropocentrism underestimate the importance of interpersonal relations. If the present ecological crisis is one small sign of the ethical, cultural and spiritual crisis of modernity, we cannot presume to heal our relationship with nature and the environment without healing all fundamental human relationships. Christian thought sees human beings as possessing a particular dignity above other creatures; it thus inculcates esteem for each person and respect for others. Our openness to others, each of whom is a "thou" capable of knowing, loving and entering into dialogue, remains the source of our nobility as human persons. A correct relationship with the created world demands that we not weaken this social dimension of openness to others, much less the transcendent dimension of our openness to the "Thou" of God. Our relationship with the environment can never be isolated from our relationship with others and with God. Otherwise, it would be nothing more than romantic individualism dressed up in ecological garb, locking us into

---

33 BENEDICT XVI, Message for the 2010 World Day of Peace, 2: AAS 102 (2010), 41.

a stifling immanence.

120. Since everything is interrelated, concern for the protection of nature is also incompatible with the justification of abortion. How can we genuinely teach the importance of concern for other vulnerable beings, however troublesome or inconvenient they may be, if we fail to protect a human embryo, even when its presence is uncomfortable and creates difficulties? "If personal and social sensitivity towards the acceptance of the new life is lost, then other forms of acceptance that are valuable for society also wither away."[34]

121. We need to develop a new synthesis capable of overcoming the false arguments of recent centuries. Christianity, in fidelity to its own identity and the rich deposit of truth which it has received from Jesus Christ, continues to reflect on these issues in fruitful dialogue with changing historical situations. In doing so, it reveals its eternal newness.

CHAPTER FOUR

Integral Ecology

137. Since everything is closely interrelated, and today's problems call for a vision capable of taking into account every aspect of the global crisis, I suggest that we now consider some elements of an integral ecology, one which clearly respects its human and social dimensions.

I. Environmental, Economic, and Social Ecology

138. Ecology studies the relationship between living organisms and the

---

34 ID., Encyclical Letter Caritas in Veritate (29 June 2009), 28: AAS 101 (2009), 663.

environment in which they develop. This necessarily entails reflection and debate about the conditions required for the life and survival of society, and the honesty needed to question certain models of development, production and consumption. It cannot be emphasized enough how everything is interconnected. Time and space are not independent of one another, and not even atoms or subatomic particles can be considered in isolation. Just as the different aspects of the planet – physical, chemical and biological – are interrelated, so too living species are part of a network which we will never fully explore and understand. A good part of our genetic code is shared by many living beings. It follows that the fragmentation of knowledge and the isolation of bits of information can actually become a form of ignorance, unless they are integrated into a broader vision of reality.

139. When we speak of the "environment," what we really mean is a relationship existing between nature and the society which lives in it. Nature cannot be regarded as something separate from ourselves or as a mere setting in which we live. We are part of nature, included in it and thus in constant interaction with it. Recognizing the reasons why a given area is polluted requires a study of the workings of society, its economy, its behavior patterns, and the ways it grasps reality. Given the scale of change, it is no longer possible to find a specific, discrete answer for each part of the problem. It is essential to seek comprehensive solutions which consider the interactions within natural systems themselves and with social systems. We are faced not with two separate crises, one environmental and the other social, but rather with one complex crisis which is both social and environmental. Strategies for a solution demand an integrated approach to combating poverty, restoring dignity to the excluded, and at the same time protecting nature.

140. Due to the number and variety of factors to be taken into account when determining the environmental impact of a concrete undertaking, it is essential to give researchers their due role, to facilitate their interaction,

and to ensure broad academic freedom. Ongoing research should also give us a better understanding of how different creatures relate to one another in making up the larger units which today we term "ecosystems." We take these systems into account not only to determine how best to use them, but also because they have an intrinsic value independent of their usefulness. Each organism, as a creature of God, is good and admirable in itself; the same is true of the harmonious ensemble of organisms existing in a defined space and functioning as a system. Although we are often not aware of it, we depend on these larger systems for our own existence. We need only recall how ecosystems interact in dispersing carbon dioxide, purifying water, controlling illnesses and epidemics, forming soil, breaking down waste, and in many other ways which we overlook or simply do not know about. Once they become conscious of this, many people realize that we live and act on the basis of a reality which has previously been given to us, which precedes our existence and our abilities. So, when we speak of "sustainable use," consideration must always be given to each ecosystem's regenerative ability in its different areas and aspects.

141. Economic growth, for its part, tends to produce predictable reactions and a certain standardization with the aim of simplifying procedures and reducing costs. This suggests the need for an "economic ecology" capable of appealing to a broader vision of reality. The protection of the environment is in fact "an integral part of the development process and cannot be considered in isolation from it."[35] We urgently need a humanism capable of bringing together the different fields of knowledge, including economics, in the service of a more integral and integrating vision. Today, the analysis of environmental problems cannot be separated from the analysis of human, family, work-related and urban contexts, nor from how individuals relate to themselves, which leads in turn to how they relate to others and to the

---

35   Rio Declaration on Environment and Development (14 June 1992), Principle 4.

environment. There is an interrelation between ecosystems and between the various spheres of social interaction, demonstrating yet again that "the whole is greater than the part."[36]

142. If everything is related, then the health of a society's institutions has consequences for the environment and the quality of human life. "Every violation of solidarity and civic friendship harms the environment."[37] In this sense, social ecology is necessarily institutional, and gradually extends to the whole of society, from the primary social group, the family, to the wider local, national and international communities. Within each social stratum, and between them, institutions develop to regulate human relationships. Anything which weakens those institutions has negative consequences, such as injustice, violence and loss of freedom. A number of countries have a relatively low level of institutional effectiveness, which results in greater problems for their people while benefiting those who profit from this situation. Whether in the administration of the state, the various levels of civil society, or relationships between individuals themselves, lack of respect for the law is becoming more common. Laws may be well framed yet remain a dead letter. Can we hope, then, that in such cases, legislation and regulations dealing with the environment will really prove effective? We know, for example, that countries which have clear legislation about the protection of forests continue to keep silent as they watch laws repeatedly being broken. Moreover, what takes place in any one area can have a direct or indirect influence on other areas. Thus, for example, drug use in affluent societies creates a continual and growing demand for products imported from poorer regions, where behavior is corrupted, lives are destroyed, and the environment continues to deteriorate.

---

36 Apostolic Exhortation Evangelii Gaudium (24 November 2013), 237: AAS 105 (2013), 1116.
37 BENEDICT XVI, Encyclical Letter Caritas in Veritate (29 June 2009), 51: AAS 101 (2009), 687.

II. Cultural Ecology

143. Together with the patrimony of nature, there is also an historic, artistic and cultural patrimony which is likewise under threat. This patrimony is a part of the shared identity of each place and a foundation upon which to build a habitable city. It is not a matter of tearing down and building new cities, supposedly more respectful of the environment yet not always more attractive to live in. Rather, there is a need to incorporate the history, culture and architecture of each place, thus preserving its original identity. Ecology, then, also involves protecting the cultural treasures of humanity in the broadest sense. More specifically, it calls for greater attention to local cultures when studying environmental problems, favouring a dialogue between scientific-technical language and the language of the people. Culture is more than what we have inherited from the past; it is also, and above all, a living, dynamic and participatory present reality, which cannot be excluded as we rethink the relationship between human beings and the environment.

144. A consumerist vision of human beings, encouraged by the mechanisms of today's globalized economy, has a levelling effect on cultures, diminishing the immense variety which is the heritage of all humanity. Attempts to resolve all problems through uniform regulations or technical interventions can lead to overlooking the complexities of local problems which demand the active participation of all members of the community. New processes taking shape cannot always fit into frameworks imported from outside; they need to be based in the local culture itself. As life and the world are dynamic realities, so our care for the world must also be flexible and dynamic. Merely technical solutions run the risk of addressing symptoms and not the more serious underlying problems. There is a need to respect the rights of peoples and cultures, and to appreciate that the

development of a social group presupposes an historical process which takes place within a cultural context and demands the constant and active involvement of local people from within their proper culture. Nor can the notion of the quality of life be imposed from without, for quality of life must be understood within the world of symbols and customs proper to each human group.

145. Many intensive forms of environmental exploitation and degradation not only exhaust the resources which provide local communities with their livelihood, but also undo the social structures which, for a long time, shaped cultural identity and their sense of the meaning of life and community. The disappearance of a culture can be just as serious, or even more serious, than the disappearance of a species of plant or animal. The imposition of a dominant lifestyle linked to a single form of production can be just as harmful as the altering of ecosystems.

146. In this sense, it is essential to show special care for indigenous communities and their cultural traditions. They are not merely one minority among others, but should be the principal dialogue partners, especially when large projects affecting their land are proposed. For them, land is not a commodity but rather a gift from God and from their ancestors who rest there, a sacred space with which they need to interact if they are to maintain their identity and values. When they remain on their land, they themselves care for it best. Nevertheless, in various parts of the world, pressure is being put on them to abandon their homelands to make room for agricultural or mining projects which are undertaken without regard for the degradation of nature and culture.

III. Ecology of Daily Life

147. Authentic development includes efforts to bring about an integral

improvement in the quality of human life, and this entails considering the setting in which people live their lives. These settings influence the way we think, feel and act. In our rooms, our homes, our workplaces and neighbourhoods, we use our environment as a way of expressing our identity. We make every effort to adapt to our environment, but when it is disorderly, chaotic or saturated with noise and ugliness, such overstimulation makes it difficult to find ourselves integrated and happy.

148. An admirable creativity and generosity is shown by persons and groups who respond to environmental limitations by alleviating the adverse effects of their surroundings and learning to orient their lives amid disorder and uncertainty. For example, in some places, where the façades of buildings are derelict, people show great care for the interior of their homes, or find contentment in the kindness and friendliness of others. A wholesome social life can light up a seemingly undesirable environment. At times a commendable human ecology is practised by the poor despite numerous hardships. The feeling of asphyxiation brought on by densely populated residential areas is countered if close and warm relationships develop, if communities are created, if the limitations of the environment are compensated for in the interior of each person who feels held within a network of solidarity and belonging. In this way, any place can turn from being a hell on earth into the setting for a dignified life.

149. The extreme poverty experienced in areas lacking harmony, open spaces or potential for integration, can lead to incidents of brutality and to exploitation by criminal organizations. In the unstable neighbourhoods of mega-cities, the daily experience of overcrowding and social anonymity can create a sense of uprootedness which spawns antisocial behavior and violence. Nonetheless, I wish to insist that love always proves more powerful. Many people in these conditions are able to weave bonds of belonging and togetherness which convert overcrowding into an experience of community in which the walls of the ego are torn down and the barriers of selfishness

overcome. This experience of a communitarian salvation often generates creative ideas for the improvement of a building or a neighbourhood.[38]

150. Given the interrelationship between living space and human behavior, those who design buildings, neighbourhoods, public spaces and cities, ought to draw on the various disciplines which help us to understand people's thought processes, symbolic language and ways of acting. It is not enough to seek the beauty of design. More precious still is the service we offer to another kind of beauty: people's quality of life, their adaptation to the environment, encounter and mutual assistance. Here too, we see how important it is that urban planning always take into consideration the views of those who will live in these areas.

151. There is also a need to protect those common areas, visual landmarks and urban landscapes which increase our sense of belonging, of rootedness, of "feeling at home" within a city which includes us and brings us together. It is important that the different parts of a city be well integrated and that those who live there have a sense of the whole, rather than being confined to one neighbourhood and failing to see the larger city as space which they share with others. Interventions which affect the urban or rural landscape should take into account how various elements combine to form a whole which is perceived by its inhabitants as a coherent and meaningful framework for their lives. Others will then no longer be seen as strangers, but as part of a "we" which all of us are working to create. For this same reason, in both urban and rural settings, it is helpful to set aside some places which can be preserved and protected from constant changes brought by human intervention.

---

38 Some authors have emphasized the values frequently found, for example, in the villas, chabolas or favelas of Latin America: cf. JUAN CARLOS SCANNONE, S.J., "La irrupción del pobre y la lógica de la gratuidad", in JUAN CARLOS SCANNONE and MARCELO PERINE (eds.), Irrupción del pobre y quehacer filosófico. Hacia una nueva racionalidad, Buenos Aires, 1993, 225- 230.

152. Lack of housing is a grave problem in many parts of the world, both in rural areas and in large cities, since state budgets usually cover only a small portion of the demand. Not only the poor, but many other members of society as well, find it difficult to own a home. Having a home has much to do with a sense of personal dignity and the growth of families. This is a major issue for human ecology. In some places, where makeshift shanty towns have sprung up, this will mean developing those neighbourhoods rather than razing or displacing them. When the poor live in unsanitary slums or in dangerous tenements, "in cases where it is necessary to relocate them, in order not to heap suffering upon suffering, adequate information needs to be given beforehand, with choices of decent housing offered, and the people directly involved must be part of the process."[39] At the same time, creativity should be shown in integrating rundown neighbourhoods into a welcoming city: "How beautiful those cities which overcome paralyzing mistrust, integrate those who are different and make this very integration a new factor of development! How attractive are those cities which, even in their architectural design, are full of spaces which connect, relate and favour the recognition of others!"[40]

153. The quality of life in cities has much to do with systems of transport, which are often a source of much suffering for those who use them. Many cars, used by one or more people, circulate in cities, causing traffic congestion, raising the level of pollution, and consuming enormous quantities of non-renewable energy. This makes it necessary to build more roads and parking areas which spoil the urban landscape. Many specialists agree on the need to give priority to public transportation. Yet some measures needed will

---

39 PONTIFICAL COUNCIL FOR JUSTICE AND PEACE, Compendium of the Social Doctrine of the Church, 482.

40 Apostolic Exhortation Evangelii Gaudium (24 November 2013), 210: AAS 105 (2013), 1107.

not prove easily acceptable to society unless substantial improvements are made in the systems themselves, which in many cities force people to put up with undignified conditions due to crowding, inconvenience, infrequent service and lack of safety.

154. Respect for our dignity as human beings often jars with the chaotic realities that people have to endure in city life. Yet this should not make us overlook the abandonment and neglect also experienced by some rural populations which lack access to essential services and where some workers are reduced to conditions of servitude, without rights or even the hope of a more dignified life.

155. Human ecology also implies another profound reality: the relationship between human life and the moral law, which is inscribed in our nature and is necessary for the creation of a more dignified environment. Pope Benedict XVI spoke of an "ecology of man," based on the fact that "man too has a nature that he must respect and that he cannot manipulate at will."[41] It is enough to recognize that our body itself establishes us in a direct relationship with the environment and with other living beings. The acceptance of our bodies as God's gift is vital for welcoming and accepting the entire world as a gift from the Father and our common home, whereas thinking that we enjoy absolute power over our own bodies turns, often subtly, into thinking that we enjoy absolute power over creation. Learning to accept our body, to care for it and to respect its fullest meaning, is an essential element of any genuine human ecology. Also, valuing one's own body in its femininity or masculinity is necessary if I am going to be able to recognize myself in an encounter with someone who is different. In this way we can joyfully accept the specific gifts of another man or woman, the work of God the Creator, and find mutual enrichment. It is not a healthy attitude which would seek "to cancel out sexual difference because it no

---

41 Address to the German Bundestag, Berlin (22 September 2011): AAS 103 (2011), 668.

longer knows how to confront it."⁴²

IV. The Principle of the Common Good

156. Human ecology is inseparable from the notion of the common good, a central and unifying principle of social ethics. The common good is "the sum of those conditions of social life which allow social groups and their individual members relatively thorough and ready access to their own fulfilment."⁴³

157. Underlying the principle of the common good is respect for the human person as such, endowed with basic and inalienable rights ordered to his or her integral development. It has also to do with the overall welfare of society and the development of a variety of intermediate groups, applying the principle of subsidiarity. Outstanding among those groups is the family, as the basic cell of society. Finally, the common good calls for social peace, the stability and security provided by a certain order which cannot be achieved without particular concern for distributive justice; whenever this is violated, violence always ensues. Society as a whole, and the state in particular, are obliged to defend and promote the common good.

158. In the present condition of global society, where injustices abound and growing numbers of people are deprived of basic human rights and considered expendable, the principle of the common good immediately becomes, logically and inevitably, a summons to solidarity and a preferential option for the poorest of our brothers and sisters. This option entails recognizing the implications of the universal destination of the world's goods, but, as I mentioned in the Apostolic Exhortation Evangelii

---

42 Catechesis (15 April 2015): L'Osservatore Romano, 16 April 2015, p. 8.
43 SECOND VATICAN ECUMENICAL COUNCIL, Pastoral Constitution on the Church in the Modern World Gaudium et Spes, 26.

Gaudium, it demands before all else an appreciation of the immense dignity of the poor in the light of our deepest convictions as believers. We need only look around us to see that, today, this option is in fact an ethical imperative essential for effectively attaining the common good.

V. Justice between the Generations

159. The notion of the common good also extends to future generations. The global economic crises have made painfully obvious the detrimental effects of disregarding our common destiny, which cannot exclude those who come after us. We can no longer speak of sustainable development apart from intergenerational solidarity. Once we start to think about the kind of world we are leaving to future generations, we look at things differently; we realize that the world is a gift which we have freely received and must share with others. Since the world has been given to us, we can no longer view reality in a purely utilitarian way, in which efficiency and productivity are entirely geared to our individual benefit. Intergenerational solidarity is not optional, but rather a basic question of justice, since the world we have received also belongs to those who will follow us. The Portuguese bishops have called upon us to acknowledge this obligation of justice: "The environment is part of a logic of receptivity. It is on loan to each generation, which must then hand it on to the next."[44] An integral ecology is marked by this broader vision.

160. What kind of world do we want to leave to those who come after us, to children who are now growing up? This question not only concerns the environment in isolation; the issue cannot be approached piecemeal. When we ask ourselves what kind of world we want to leave behind, we

---

44 PORTUGUESE BISHOPS' CONFERENCE, Pastoral Letter Responsabilidade Solidária pelo
Bem Comum (15 September 2003), 20.

think in the first place of its general direction, its meaning and its values. Unless we struggle with these deeper issues, I do not believe that our concern for ecology will produce significant results. But if these issues are courageously faced, we are led inexorably to ask other pointed questions: What is the purpose of our life in this world? Why are we here? What is the goal of our work and all our efforts? What need does the earth have of us? It is no longer enough, then, simply to state that we should be concerned for future generations. We need to see that what is at stake is our own dignity. Leaving an inhabitable planet to future generations is, first and foremost, up to us. The issue is one which dramatically affects us, for it has to do with the ultimate meaning of our earthly sojourn.

161. Doomsday predictions can no longer be met with irony or disdain. We may well be leaving to coming generations debris, desolation and filth. The pace of consumption, waste and environmental change has so stretched the planet's capacity that our contemporary lifestyle, unsustainable as it is, can only precipitate catastrophes, such as those which even now periodically occur in different areas of the world. The effects of the present imbalance can only be reduced by our decisive action, here and now. We need to reflect on our accountability before those who will have to endure the dire consequences.

162. Our difficulty in taking up this challenge seriously has much to do with an ethical and cultural decline which has accompanied the deterioration of the environment. Men and women of our postmodern world run the risk of rampant individualism, and many problems of society are connected with today's self-centerd culture of instant gratification. We see this in the crisis of family and social ties and the difficulties of recognizing the other. Parents can be prone to impulsive and wasteful consumption, which then affects their children who find it increasingly difficult to acquire a home of their own and build a family. Furthermore, our inability to think seriously about future generations is linked to our inability to broaden the scope of our

present interests and to give consideration to those who remain excluded from development. Let us not only keep the poor of the future in mind, but also today's poor, whose life on this earth is brief and who cannot keep on waiting. Hence, "in addition to a fairer sense of intergenerational solidarity there is also an urgent moral need for a renewed sense of intragenerational solidarity."[45]

IV. Politics and Economy in Dialogue for Human Fulfilment

189. Politics must not be subject to the economy, nor should the economy be subject to the dictates of an efficiency-driven paradigm of technocracy. Today, in view of the common good, there is urgent need for politics and economics to enter into a frank dialogue in the service of life, especially human life. Saving banks at any cost, making the public pay the price, foregoing a firm commitment to reviewing and reforming the entire system, only reaffirms the absolute power of a financial system, a power which has no future and will only give rise to new crises after a slow, costly and only apparent recovery. The financial crisis of 2007-08 provided an opportunity to develop a new economy, more attentive to ethical principles, and new ways of regulating speculative financial practices and virtual wealth. But the response to the crisis did not include rethinking the outdated criteria which continue to rule the world. Production is not always rational, and is usually tied to economic variables which assign to products a value that does not necessarily correspond to their real worth. This frequently leads to an overproduction of some commodities, with unnecessary impact on the environment and with negative results on regional economies. The financial bubble also tends to be a productive bubble. The problem of the real economy is not confronted with vigour, yet it is the real economy which

---

45 BENEDICT XVI, Message for the 2010 World Day of Peace, 8: AAS 102 (2010), 45.

makes diversification and improvement in production possible, helps companies to function well, and enables small and medium businesses to develop and create employment.

190. Here too, it should always be kept in mind that "environmental protection cannot be assured solely on the basis of financial calculations of costs and benefits. The environment is one of those goods that cannot be adequately safeguarded or promoted by market forces."[46] Once more, we need to reject a magical conception of the market, which would suggest that problems can be solved simply by an increase in the profits of companies or individuals. Is it realistic to hope that those who are obsessed with maximizing profits will stop to reflect on the environmental damage which they will leave behind for future generations? Where profits alone count, there can be no thinking about the rhythms of nature, its phases of decay and regeneration, or the complexity of ecosystems which may be gravely upset by human intervention. Moreover, biodiversity is considered at most a deposit of economic resources available for exploitation, with no serious thought for the real value of things, their significance for persons and cultures, or the concerns and needs of the poor.

191. Whenever these questions are raised, some react by accusing others of irrationally attempting to stand in the way of progress and human development. But we need to grow in the conviction that a decrease in the pace of production and consumption can at times give rise to another form of progress and development. Efforts to promote a sustainable use of natural resources are not a waste of money, but rather an investment capable of providing other economic benefits in the medium term. If we look at the larger picture, we can see that more diversified and innovative forms of production which impact less on the environment can prove very profitable. It is a matter of openness to different possibilities which do

---

46 PONTIFICAL COUNCIL FOR JUSTICE AND PEACE, Compendium of the Social Doctrine of the Church, 470.

not involve stifling human creativity and its ideals of progress, but rather directing that energy along new channels.

192. For example, a path of productive development, which is more creative and better directed, could correct the present disparity between excessive technological investment in consumption and insufficient investment in resolving urgent problems facing the human family. It could generate intelligent and profitable ways of reusing, revamping and recycling, and it could also improve the energy efficiency of cities. Productive diversification offers the fullest possibilities to human ingenuity to create and innovate, while at the same time protecting the environment and creating more sources of employment. Such creativity would be a worthy expression of our most noble human qualities, for we would be striving intelligently, boldly and responsibly to promote a sustainable and equitable development within the context of a broader concept of quality of life. On the other hand, to find ever new ways of despoiling nature, purely for the sake of new consumer items and quick profit, would be, in human terms, less worthy and creative, and more superficial.

193. In any event, if in some cases sustainable development were to involve new forms of growth, then in other cases, given the insatiable and irresponsible growth produced over many decades, we need also to think of containing growth by setting some reasonable limits and even retracing our steps before it is too late. We know how unsustainable is the behavior of those who constantly consume and destroy, while others are not yet able to live in a way worthy of their human dignity. That is why the time has come to accept decreased growth in some parts of the world, in order to provide resources for other places to experience healthy growth. Benedict XVI has said that "technologically advanced societies must be prepared to encourage more sober lifestyles, while reducing their energy consumption and improving its efficiency."[47]

---

47 Message for the 2010 World Day of Peace, 9: AAS 102 (2010), 46.

194. For new models of progress to arise, there is a need to change "models of global development";[48] this will entail a responsible reflection on "the meaning of the economy and its goals with an eye to correcting its malfunctions and misapplications."[49] It is not enough to balance, in the medium term, the protection of nature with financial gain, or the preservation of the environment with progress. Halfway measures simply delay the inevitable disaster. Put simply, it is a matter of redefining our notion of progress. A technological and economic development which does not leave in its wake a better world and an integrally higher quality of life cannot be considered progress. Frequently, in fact, people's quality of life actually diminishes – by the deterioration of the environment, the low quality of food or the depletion of resources – in the midst of economic growth. In this context, talk of sustainable growth usually becomes a way of distracting attention and offering excuses. It absorbs the language and values of ecology into the categories of finance and technocracy, and the social and environmental responsibility of businesses often gets reduced to a series of marketing and image-enhancing measures.

195. The principle of the maximization of profits, frequently isolated from other considerations, reflects a misunderstanding of the very concept of the economy. As long as production is increased, little concern is given to whether it is at the cost of future resources or the health of the environment; as long as the clearing of a forest increases production, no one calculates the losses entailed in the desertification of the land, the harm done to biodiversity or the increased pollution. In a word, businesses profit by calculating and paying only a fraction of the costs involved. Yet only when "the economic and social costs of using up shared environmental resources are recognized with transparency and fully borne by those who

---

48 Ibid.

49 Ibid., 5: p. 43.

incur them, not by other peoples or future generations,"[50] can those actions be considered ethical. An instrumental way of reasoning, which provides a purely static analysis of realities in the service of present needs, is at work whether resources are allocated by the market or by state central planning.

196. What happens with politics? Let us keep in mind the principle of subsidiarity, which grants freedom to develop the capabilities present at every level of society, while also demanding a greater sense of responsibility for the common good from those who wield greater power. Today, it is the case that some economic sectors exercise more power than states themselves. But economics without politics cannot be justified, since this would make it impossible to favour other ways of handling the various aspects of the present crisis. The mindset which leaves no room for sincere concern for the environment is the same mindset which lacks concern for the inclusion of the most vulnerable members of society. For "the current model, with its emphasis on success and self-reliance, does not appear to favour an investment in efforts to help the slow, the weak or the less talented to find opportunities in life."[51]

197. What is needed is a politics which is far-sighted and capable of a new, integral and interdisciplinary approach to handling the different aspects of the crisis. Often, politics itself is responsible for the disrepute in which it is held, on account of corruption and the failure to enact sound public policies. If in a given region the state does not carry out its responsibilities, some business groups can come forward in the guise of benefactors, wield real power, and consider themselves exempt from certain rules, to the point of tolerating different forms of organized crime, human trafficking, the drug trade and violence, all of which become very difficult to eradicate.

---

50   BENEDICT XVI, Encyclical Letter Caritas in Veritate (29 June 2009), 50: AAS 101 (2009), 686.
51   Apostolic Exhortation Evangelii Gaudium (24 November 2013), 209: AAS 105 (2013), 1107.

If politics shows itself incapable of breaking such a perverse logic, and remains caught up in inconsequential discussions, we will continue to avoid facing the major problems of humanity. A strategy for real change calls for rethinking processes in their entirety, for it is not enough to include a few superficial ecological considerations while failing to question the logic which underlies present-day culture. A healthy politics needs to be able to take up this challenge.

198. Politics and the economy tend to blame each other when it comes to poverty and environmental degradation. It is to be hoped that they can acknowledge their own mistakes and find forms of interaction directed to the common good. While some are concerned only with financial gain, and others with holding on to or increasing their power, what we are left with are conflicts or spurious agreements where the last thing either party is concerned about is caring for the environment and protecting those who are most vulnerable. Here too, we see how true it is that "unity is greater than conflict."[52]

CHAPTER SIX

Ecological Education and Spirituality

202. Many things have to change course, but it is we human beings above all who need to change. We lack an awareness of our common origin, of our mutual belonging, and of a future to be shared with everyone. This basic awareness would enable the development of new convictions, attitudes and forms of life. A great cultural, spiritual and educational challenge stands before us, and it will demand that we set out on the long path of renewal.

---

52 Ibid., 228: AAS 105 (2013), 1113.

I. Toward a New Lifestyle

203. Since the market tends to promote extreme consumerism in an effort to sell its products, people can easily get caught up in a whirlwind of needless buying and spending. Compulsive consumerism is one example of how the techno-economic paradigm affects individuals. Romano Guardini had already foreseen this: "The gadgets and technics forced upon him by the patterns of machine production and of abstract planning mass man accepts quite simply; they are the forms of life itself. To either a greater or lesser degree mass man is convinced that his conformity is both reasonable and just."[53] This paradigm leads people to believe that they are free as long as they have the supposed freedom to consume. But those really free are the minority who wield economic and financial power. Amid this confusion, postmodern humanity has not yet achieved a new self-awareness capable of offering guidance and direction, and this lack of identity is a source of anxiety. We have too many means and only a few insubstantial ends.

204. The current global situation engenders a feeling of instability and uncertainty, which in turn becomes "a seedbed for collective selfishness."[54] When people become self-centerd and self- enclosed, their greed increases. The emptier a person's heart is, the more he or she needs things to buy, own and consume. It becomes almost impossible to accept the limits imposed by reality. In this horizon, a genuine sense of the common good also disappears. As these attitudes become more widespread, social norms are respected only to the extent that they do not clash with personal needs. So our concern cannot be limited merely to the threat of extreme weather events, but must also extend to the catastrophic consequences of social unrest. Obsession with a consumerist lifestyle, above all when few

---

53   ROMANO GUARDINI, Das Ende der Neuzeit, 9th edition, Würzburg, 1965, 66-67 (English: The End of the Modern World, Wilmington, 1998, 60).

54   JOHN PAUL II, Message for the 1990 World Day of Peace, 1: AAS 82 (1990), 147.

people are capable of maintaining it, can only lead to violence and mutual destruction.

205. Yet all is not lost. Human beings, while capable of the worst, are also capable of rising above themselves, choosing again what is good, and making a new start, despite their mental and social conditioning. We are able to take an honest look at ourselves, to acknowledge our deep dissatisfaction, and to embark on new paths to authentic freedom. No system can completely suppress our openness to what is good, true and beautiful, or our God-given ability to respond to his grace at work deep in our hearts. I appeal to everyone throughout the world not to forget this dignity which is ours. No one has the right to take it from us.

206. A change in lifestyle could bring healthy pressure to bear on those who wield political, economic and social power. This is what consumer movements accomplish by boycotting certain products. They prove successful in changing the way businesses operate, forcing them to consider their environmental footprint and their patterns of production. When social pressure affects their earnings, businesses clearly have to find ways to produce differently. This shows us the great need for a sense of social responsibility on the part of consumers. "Purchasing is always a moral – and not simply economic – act."[55] Today, in a word, "the issue of environmental degradation challenges us to examine our lifestyle."[56]

207. The Earth Charter asked us to leave behind a period of self-destruction and make a new start, but we have not as yet developed a universal awareness needed to achieve this. Here, I would echo that courageous challenge: "As never before in history, common destiny beckons us to seek a new beginning... Let ours be a time remembered for the awakening

---

55 BENEDICT XVI, Encyclical Letter Caritas in Veritate (29 June 2009), 66: AAS 101 (2009), 699.
56 D., Message for the 2010 World Day of Peace, 11: AAS 102 (2010), 48.

of a new reverence for life, the firm resolve to achieve sustainability, the quickening of the struggle for justice and peace, and the joyful celebration of life."[57]

208. We are always capable of going out of ourselves towards the other. Unless we do this, other creatures will not be recognized for their true worth; we are unconcerned about caring for things for the sake of others; we fail to set limits on ourselves in order to avoid the suffering of others or the deterioration of our surroundings. Disinterested concern for others, and the rejection of every form of self-centeredness and self-absorption, are essential if we truly wish to care for our brothers and sisters and for the natural environment. These attitudes also attune us to the moral imperative of assessing the impact of our every action and personal decision on the world around us. If we can overcome individualism, we will truly be able to develop a different lifestyle and bring about significant changes in society.

II. Educating for the Convenant between Humanity and the Environment

209. An awareness of the gravity of today's cultural and ecological crisis must be translated into new habits. Many people know that our current progress and the mere amassing of things and pleasures are not enough to give meaning and joy to the human heart, yet they feel unable to give up what the market sets before them. In those countries which should be making the greatest changes in consumer habits, young people have a new ecological sensitivity and a generous spirit, and some of them are making admirable efforts to protect the environment. At the same time, they have grown up in a milieu of extreme consumerism and affluence which makes it difficult to develop other habits. We are faced with an educational challenge.

---

57 Earth Charter, The Hague (29 June 2000).

210. Environmental education has broadened its goals. Whereas in the beginning it was mainly centerd on scientific information, consciousness-raising and the prevention of environmental risks, it tends now to include a critique of the "myths" of a modernity grounded in a utilitarian mindset (individualism, unlimited progress, competition, consumerism, the unregulated market). It seeks also to restore the various levels of ecological equilibrium, establishing harmony within ourselves, with others, with nature and other living creatures, and with God. Environmental education should facilitate making the leap towards the transcendent which gives ecological ethics its deepest meaning. It needs educators capable of developing an ethics of ecology, and helping people, through effective pedagogy, to grow in solidarity, responsibility and compassionate care.

211. Yet this education, aimed at creating an "ecological citizenship," is at times limited to providing information, and fails to instil good habits. The existence of laws and regulations is insufficient in the long run to curb bad conduct, even when effective means of enforcement are present. If the laws are to bring about significant, long-lasting effects, the majority of the members of society must be adequately motivated to accept them, and personally transformed to respond.

Only by cultivating sound virtues will people be able to make a selfless ecological commitment. A person who could afford to spend and consume more but regularly uses less heating and wears warmer clothes, shows the kind of convictions and attitudes which help to protect the environment. There is a nobility in the duty to care for creation through little daily actions, and it is wonderful how education can bring about real changes in lifestyle. Education in environmental responsibility can encourage ways of acting which directly and significantly affect the world around us, such as avoiding the use of plastic and paper, reducing water consumption, separating refuse, cooking only what can reasonably be consumed, showing care for other living beings, using public transport or car-pooling, planting trees, turning off unnecessary lights, or any number of other practices. All of these reflect a generous and worthy creativity which brings out the best in human beings. Reusing something instead of immediately discarding it, when done for the right reasons, can be an act of love which expresses our own dignity.

212. We must not think that these efforts are not going to change the world. They benefit society, often unbeknown to us, for they call forth a goodness which, albeit unseen, inevitably tends to spread. Furthermore, such actions can restore our sense of self-esteem; they can enable us to live more fully and to feel that life on earth is worthwhile.

213. Ecological education can take place in a variety of settings: at school, in families, in the media, in catechesis and elsewhere. Good education plants seeds when we are young, and these continue to bear fruit throughout life. Here, though, I would stress the great importance of the family, which is "the place in which life – the gift of God – can be properly welcomed and protected against the many attacks to which it is exposed, and can develop in accordance with what constitutes authentic human growth. In the face of the so-called culture of death, the family is the heart of the culture of life."[58] In the family we first learn how to show love and respect for life; we are taught the proper use of things, order and cleanliness, respect for the local ecosystem and care for all creatures. In the family we receive an integral education, which enables us to grow harmoniously in personal maturity. In the family we learn to ask without demanding, to say "thank you" as an expression of genuine gratitude for what we have been given, to control our aggressivity and greed, and to ask forgiveness when we have caused harm. These simple gestures of heartfelt courtesy help to create a culture of shared life and respect for our surroundings.

---

58 JOHN PAUL II, Encyclical Letter Centesimus Annus (1 May 1991), 39: AAS 83 (1991), 842.

214. Political institutions and various other social groups are also entrusted with helping to raise people's awareness. So too is the Church. All Christian communities have an important role to play in ecological education. It is my hope that our seminaries and houses of formation will provide an education in responsible simplicity of life, in grateful contemplation of God's world, and in concern for the needs of the poor and the protection of the environment. Because the stakes are so high, we need institutions empowered to impose penalties for damage inflicted on the environment. But we also need the personal qualities of self-control and willingness to learn from one another.

215. In this regard, "the relationship between a good aesthetic education and the maintenance of a healthy environment cannot be overlooked."[59] By learning to see and appreciate beauty, we learn to reject self-interested pragmatism. If someone has not learned to stop and admire something beautiful, we should not be surprised if he or she treats everything as an object to be used and abused without scruple. If we want to bring about deep change, we need to realize that certain mindsets really do influence our behavior. Our efforts at education will be inadequate and ineffectual unless we strive to promote a new way of thinking about human beings, life, society and our relationship with nature. Otherwise, the paradigm of consumerism will continue to advance, with the help of the media and the highly effective workings of the market.

---

59   ID., Message for the 1990 World Day of Peace, 14: AAS 82 (1990), 155.

Some Thoughts from Pope Francis

Sources

The reader should note that all the thoughts expressed in this book are excerpted from longer texts. For a full understanding of Pope Francis's thoughts, the context of the entire text should be considered. All sources here are available on the Internet at http://w2.vatican.va/content/francesco/en.html

Thoughts titled Grassroot Organizations, Solidarity, Social Activists, Altruism and Hypocrisy, Land, Housing, Real Estate, Slums, Work, Exploitation, the Value of Workers, Discarding people, Unemployment, Peace and Ecology, the War Industry, the Plunder of Nature, the Worship of Money, Integrating the Local and the Global, Remedying the Causes of Poverty, Irksome Discourse, Market Forces, Politicians, Global Economics, Papal Interest, the defense of Spcies, the nature of Peace, Time and Space, Ideas and Realities, Relations with Islam, Embracing Muslims, Mary, Globalization and Localization, and Grassroots Movements are from Pope Francis's Address to a Meeting of Popular Movements, Old Synod Hall, October 28, 2014.

Thoughts on the Cost of Consumerism, the Loss of Happiness, the Spreading of Goodness, the Power of God's Word, the Economy of Exclusion, People as Leftovers, Trickle-Down Economics, the Financial Crisis, the Wealth Gap, Ethics, Inequality, Religious Freedom, Superficial Culture, Rejection of the Transcendent, the Culture Crisis within Families, Urban Crime, Christian Service, Liberation Communication, the Quest for Sprituality, Talk, the Liberation and Promotion of the Poor, the Social Function of Property, and the Rights of All Peoples are from his apostolic exhortation Evangelii Gaudium.

Be Revolutionary

On Labor Disparity is from his address to the Pontifical Council for Peace and Justice, October 2, 2014.

On the Elderly is from his Address to the Elderly at St. Peter's Square, September 28, 2014.

On Religious Freedom, Attitudes for Religious Freedom, is from his Address to Leaders of Other Religions and Other Christian Denominations, September 21, 2015.

On Fear of Freedom is from Te Deum and Celebration of First Vespers of the Solemnity of Mary, Mother of God, Vatican Basilica, December 31, 2014

On Migrants and Refugees is from his message for the 101st World Day of Migrants and Refugees in 2015.

On Slaves and On the Causes of Slavery came from his Message for the Celebration of World Day of Peace, "No Longer Slaves, but Brothers and Sisters, January 1, 2015.

On the Seeking of Truth and On Religious Freedom are from his Address to Participants in the Conference on International Religious Freedom and the Global Clash of Values, Consistory Hall, June 20, 2014.

On Financial Markets is from his Address to the Conference on "Impact Investing for the Poor," promoted by the Pontifical Council for Justice and Peace.

On Legacy and On the Courage to Make Peace are from his Invocation for Peace, Vatican Gardens, June 8, 2014.

On Expectations of the G20 is from A Letter to the Prime Minister of Australia on the Occasion of the G20 summit, Brisbane, November 15, 2014.

On ISIS is from his Letter to the General Secretary of the United Nations Concerning the Situation in Northern Iraq, August 9, 2014.

Some Thoughts from Pope Francis

On Global Warming is from his Message on the Occasion of the 20th Conference of the Parties of the United Nations Framework Convention on Climate Change, December 1, 2014.

On Dialogue with Other Religions is from his Address to a Meeting Sponsored by the Pontifical Institute for Arabic and Islamic Studies, January 24, 2015.

On Grandparents is from his address to the National Numerous Family Association, December 28, 2014.

On the Olympics is from his Address to the Leaders and Athletes of the Italian National Olympic Committee, December 19, 2014.

On Hidden Slavery is from his address at the ceremony for the signing of the Faith Leader's Universal Declaration against Slavery, December 2, 2015.

On Islamophobia, On Christianophobia, On Prayer in a Mosque, On the Ongoing Third World War, and On Atomic Weapons are from an inflight press conference held between Istanbul and Rome on November 30, 2014.

On Middle East Peace is from a meeting with the president, prime minister and civil authorities of Turkey, November 28, 2014.

On Hunger and On Solidarity and Hunger are from his address to the FAO at the 2nd International Conference on Nutrition, November 20, 2014.

On the Concept of Person, On Dignity and Economic Interests, On Individual Rights and Duties, On Lonliness, On Transcendence of Heaven and Earth, On Stewardship of Nature, and On Christians as a Soul are from his address to the European Parliament, November 25, 2014.

On Experimentation with Life is from his Address to the Conference of the Italian Catholic Physicians' Association, November 15, 2014.

Be Revolutionary

On Economy and Finance is from his address to the World Congress of Accountants, November 14, 2014.

On Religious Diversity is from his address to a plenary session of the Pontifical Council for Interreligious Dialogue, November 28, 2015.

On Rugby is from his address to the Italian and Argentine Rugby Teams, November 22, 2014.

On Torture and On Stopping Aggressors are from an inflight press conference between Korea and Rome, August 18, 2014.

On Diplomacy and On the Work of Justice are from his Address to Authorities at Chungmu Hall at the "Blue House" in Seoul, August 14, 2014.

On Cultivation and On Playing with Children are from his Address to the World of Labor and Industry, University of Molise, Campobasso, Italy, July 5, 2014.

On Unemployment is from an inflight interview with journalists between the Holy Land and Rome, May 26, 2014.

On Pilgrims is from his Address on a Visit to the Grand Mufti of Jerusalem, in Jersalem, on May 26, 2014.

On Learning and On Education are from his Address to Students and Teachers from Schools across Italy, May 10, 2014.

On Hope is from his address to the Italian Conference of Secular Institutes, May 10, 2014.

On Homosexuality and On Jorge Mario Bergoglio are from "Interview with Pope Francis," by Fr. Antonio Spadaro.

On Soccer is from his Address to the Fiorentina and Napoli Soccer Teams and a Delegation of the Soccer Federation and the Series A League, May 2, 2014.

Some Thoughts from Pope Francis

On Healthcare is from his Address to a Conference of the Italian Socity of Surgical Oncology, April 12, 2014.

On the Right to Life and On Economy and Morality are from the Italian Pro-Life Movement, April 11, 2014.

On the Abuse of Children by Priests, On Educational Experimentation, and On New Culture are from his Address to the International Catholic Child Bureau, April 11, 2014.

On Human Trafficking is from his Address to the International Conference on Combating Human Trafficking, April 1, 2014.

On Mayors is from his Address to an Association of Municipal Leaders of Italy, April 5, 2014.

On His Own Happiness is from his Address to a Group of Young People from Belgium, March 31, 2014.

On Work and On Unemployment are from his Address to Managers and Workers of the Terni Steel Mill and the Faithful of Diocese of Terni-Narni-Amelia, Italy, March 20, 2014.

On marriage Forever is from his Address to Engaged Couples Preparing for Marriage, February 14, 2014.

Be Revolutionary

Some Thoughts from Pope Francis

About Pope Francis

Born Jorge Mario Bergoglio on December 17, 1936 in Buenos Aires, Argentina, He is the eldest of five children born to an Italian father and Argentinian mother who was also of Italian parentage. Before entering the Society of Jesus, he worked briefly as a bar bouncer, a janitor, and chemical technician.

Bergoglio was named Bishop of Rome in 2013 following the resignation of Pope Benedict XVI. He chose his papal name — Francisco in Spanish and Italian — in honor of St. Francis of Assisi for that saint's love of peace, the poor, and nature. He is the first pope to take that name. He is also the first Jesuit to become pope and the first pope from Latin America or the southern hemisphere.

On his first days as pope, Francis indicated that his papacy would be marked by concern for the poor and downtrodden. After his election, he took a public bus back to his hotel. A few days later, on Holy Thursday, he washed and kissed the feet of male and female prisoners — one of them a Muslim — as a sign that he considered himself at their service. While this humble gesture is a tradition among popes, it was the first time it was performed for a woman or a non-Catholic.

Francis is fluent in Spanish, Latin, and Italian and can also understand English, French, German, Portuguese, and Ukrainian.

Be Revolutionary

About Sister Barbara Staley

Sr. Barbara Staley has been a Missionary Sister of the Sacred Heart since 1988. She has a bachelor's degree in Education from Clarion University of Pennsylvania and a Masters of Social York from New York University. She has worked with many poor and marginalized populations within the United States and abroad. Her work has included working with the developmentally disabled in residential care settings, providing counselling to street children in New York City, helping undocumented immigrants with accessing health care and social services in Chicago, providing mental health services to the mentally ill and to persons with addictions, activities of human promotion in Guatemala, and establishing a clinic in the outback of Swaziland to help persons with HIV, their families, and orphans.

Sister Barbara currently serves as the Superior General of her religious congregation. The organization of women religious, which has borne the missionary legacy of St. Frances Xavier Cabrini since 1880, is active in 15 countries on six continents. For more information, see mothercabrini.org or msccabrini.org . For more on Sr. Barbara's work in Swaziland, see Cabriniministries.org .

Some Thoughts from Pope Francis

About Glenn Alan Cheney

Glenn Alan Cheney is a writer, journalist, translator, and editor. He has degrees in philosophy, communication, English, and creative writing. The author of over 25 books, he has written on Chernobyl, Brazil, environmental issues, nuns, Swaziland, Abraham Lincoln, Machado de Assis, accountancy, the Pilgrims, Brazil's Quilombo dos Palmares, nuclear proliferation, Mohandas Gandhi, and many other topics. He also writes fiction, poetry, and op-ed essays. He lives in Hanover, Conn.

www.ingramcontent.com/pod-product-compliance
Lightning Source LLC
Chambersburg PA
CBHW020612300426
44113CB00007B/618